ENDORSEMENTS FOR BRAVE WOMEN AT WORK: LESSONS IN LEADERSHIP

"I highly recommend this book to anyone who is interested in learning more about ways to manage, or who wants to read a powerful and inspirational story of overcoming fears and obstacles that you may face. This book will touch your heart, challenge your mind, and uplift your spirit. It is a testament to the human capacity for growth and transformation, and a reminder that we are not alone in our struggles."

—BEATA DOWLING

"Authored by a diverse group of remarkable women, "Brave Women at Work Lessons in Leadership" is a testament to the power of personal narratives in shaping leadership philosophies. It is an unapologetic embrace of vulnerability and inspiration. These women share their triumphs and candidly disclose their failures and setbacks. Through their honesty, they illuminate the path toward genuine leadership— one that celebrates authenticity, empathy, and inclusivity."

—CATHY SKALA

"Touching on organizational agility, self-directed problem solving and loaded with the motivational, inspiring true-life journeys of true women leaders, it's a fast & intelligent read. I feel more capable of leading with authenticity and driving influential interactions after highlighting and dog-earing all the memorable moments within!"

—GEORGE FISCUS

"After reading *Brave Women at Work: Lessons in Leadership*, I am reminded of the famous Dolly Parton quote: 'If your actions create a legacy that inspires others to dream more, learn more, do more and become more, then, you are an excellent leader.' This book is the inspiration and instruction I wish I would have had earlier in my career."

—GAIL LEMON-ZONA

"As a young professional in the corporate world looking for strong leadership examples, this book provided that and so much more. As I read through the materials, I felt a sense of trust and a connection to the contributors as they went over life lessons from handling imposter syndrome to learning when a role and place is not meant for you. I will be sharing this book with all my male and female co-workers."

—CASSANDRA RUTHE

"Let this book be your compass, your catalyst for growth or your motivation for a crowning achievement. Allow these stories to embolden your leadership with authenticity, insight, and unwavering determination. These are stories of challenges, choice and courage. These lived experiences shared by extraordinary women will stir your spirt and invite you to unlock and unleash your everyday brave."

—TERI BUMP

"An invaluable playbook for navigating the corporate land-scape, this insightful collection of diverse stories offers wisdom and inspiration for anyone facing challenges in the professional world. Through its engaging storytelling format, this book serves as a manual for decision-mak-ing and empowers women and all underdogs to survive, thrive and excel- appreciate the gift from these authors!"

—KEVIN THOMPSON

"This book is a great platform for the thousands of women leaders out there with stories and lessons to share. With each chapter having its own spin based on background and experience every story will resonate differently, providing something for everyone. I hope to see (and maybe contrib-ute to!) more collections of stories like this in the future."

—TIFFANY THOMPSON

"There are numerous inspirational texts written, this one stands out by sharing candid heartfelt stories."

—SHARON ROBERSON

"I would recommend that any woman interested in growing in her leadership abilities spend some time with this book. These authors' stories are candid and engaging and contain actionable advice on developing one's own leadership abilities. I resonated with the collection's overarching message that strong leadership is about authenticity and embracing who we are—any woman can leverage her natural abilities to become an effective leader. As a young professional seeking to grow as a leader, I find these stories to be both helpful and empowering."

—BRIANA MAUND

"A brilliant collection and exploration of real and honest life experiences of women in leadership. This book provides invaluable guidance that invites readers to embrace authenticity, diversity and empathy in their own lives as they lead in their professional and personal worlds. The feminine perspective is compelling and inspirational while being relatable to all who read these stories. This book makes me proud to be a woman in leadership."

—AMANDA JAMES

"In a world where most models of leadership are defined by men, this book affirms and validates women's ways of leading. Inspirational. Authentic. Honest. And, grace-filled. The women authors tell their stories, in their own words, in their own ways and, in doing so, advocate, support and uplift women leaders. It is a must-read for all women, particularly those who doubt their leadership given the male models of leadership that permeate all industries. Share this book with every girl and woman you know because we need to change the paradigm. We also need to elevate women leaders!"

—PATRICIA PERILLO

"A pragmatic and inspirational collection of essays from women in a variety of fields that shares the personal and professional challenges encountered and support received as they navigated their career paths. While no two avenues were the same, the women endorsed many similar inherent and learned traits necessary for rising to leadership roles. This collection offers excellent advice to all who wish to prosper in their vocation."

—GLORIA JONES

"Natalie Benamou shares her story of resilience and transformation, and she recovers from a life changing accident, becomes part of a global women's network which opens her eyes to the collective power of women to help each other and moves through the challenges of leadership to discover her true purpose. In this completed narrative, we witness her pivotal moment on January 9, 202 as she orchestrates the groundbreaking EmpowHer networking event, setting the stage for profound change. In a world of uncertainty, Natalie's story reminds us to listen to our hearts, embrace adversity, and forge ahead with purpose. Discover the transformative power of resilience and the boundless potential within each of us."

—WENDY WHITE

"The "Meet the Moment" piece was quite dramatic and engaging. It was emotional to accompany the author as she met each moment. The authenticity and care shown for others during the seminal decision points was awe-inspiring. The personal-internal resources, leadership principles and practices that it took to work through these moments of adversity highlight tools that we all should consider for our leadership journeys."

—M. WATERS

"A journey of personal and professional determination is an account by Natalie Robinson, an amazing leader who reveals her difficulties and reflections that made me nod my head in agreement as I could relate to similar examples in my life. In her leadership story, Natalie shares her experiences of overcoming the challenges and obstacles that she faced not only in her professional life but her early years that helped define her characteristics as a teammate and leader, and how ultimately found healing and happiness through her experiences.

Her writing style is honest, engaging, and emotional, never shying away from the difficult and painful aspects of her journey. She also shows how she was able to find hope and joy in the midst of her struggles, and how she developed a positive and empowering mindset."

—BEATA DOWLING

BRAVE
WOMEN
AT WORK

Lessons in Leadership

BRAVE WOMEN AT WORK

Lessons in Leadership

JENNIFER PESTIKAS

Managing Editor

HOPE MUELLER

Contributors:

- Mylene Barizo
- Natalie Benamou
- Churni Bhattacharya
- Ronicka Briscoe
- Shelia Higgs Burkhalter
- Echell Eady
- Jennifer Pestikas
- M.L. Cissy Petty
- Mary Beth Ritchey
- Natalie Robinson

Hunter Street
Press

Brave Women at Work

Copyright © Hope Mueller, Hunter Street Press

ISBN: 978-1-7372751-3-8 (Hardcover)
ISBN: 978-1-7372751-2-1 (eBook)

CONTENTS

INTRODUCTION

Early in my career I read every business book that I could get my hands on. A few years out of college an admired female leader told me I had natural leadership abilities, and I was being considered for a supervisory role. She sent me to the career development center; and although I did not get the position we discussed, the offer sparked my interest and was my initiation into learning everything there was available about leadership.

Business books littered my nightstand as I furiously took notes. I swiftly deployed these ideas and suggestions. Then I learned that the techniques found in leadership books written by men don't always work for women. A confident woman introducing herself with a firm handshake and direct eye contact does not necessarily work the same way it does for men. I was told *not to do* exactly that. I was told I was too confident; and when I asked for an example, the instance was that I introduced myself to a Vice President.

As I read these professional women's stories, I realized this was the business book I needed in those early days. This is a leadership book written by women, and the reader learns about different styles of leadership. Women adjust their approaches to fit the circumstances. They often must understand the broader view and use creative means to accomplish their leadership objectives—direct eye contact and a confident delivery may not always work.

These shared stories are from a group of incredible female leaders, executives, and industry leaders. Through trial, error, and setbacks, these women reflected on their challenges, then got to work to solve and overcome them. These women consistently applied a mix of collaboration, clear expectations, cheerleading, and service leadership.

You will read about the recipe of leadership, hear from self-proclaimed introverted leaders, and acquire key learning and critical components to consider for your own style and brand of leadership. The authors share personal stories and important leadership lessons that every reader can learn from and incorporate into their own lives and careers.

In a word these women are advocates. They advocate for their team members, their organizations, and for themselves. Through their concerted and pointed efforts, they are improving the professional world for women. Entertaining, inspiring, and soulful—this is the business book we all need.

INTRODUCING NATALIE ROBINSON

Natalie Robinson is an accomplished senior leader with over nineteen years of experience in the pharmaceutical-biotech industry. As a visionary leader, she brings an enterprise approach to her role, focusing on strategy development and execution. Natalie's passion for leading people and impacting the business is evident in her inspiring and impactful leadership style. She is best known for her exceptional leadership skills, which have earned her multiple nominations as leader of the year, ultimately winning the prestigious award in 2020. With expertise in human development, sales, marketing, market access, analytics, and matrix management, Natalie is a professional with a track record of success. Her ability to navigate complex business challenges and drive organizational growth furthers her reputation as an esteemed leader in the industry.

HEAD UP, EYES OPEN, HEART CENTERED

The sweat rolls down my face and stings my eyes. Twisting the front of my jersey I bend to wipe my brow, but the drenched cloth provides little relief. The air sits hot and heavy, not moving, thick with humidity. This is Texas in summer.

It's the championship game and our fifth game of the weekend. After a grueling ninety-minutes of play we tack on thirty extra minutes of overtime to try and break the tie. The final whistle blows and there is no change to the scoreboard, so penalty kicks will decide the championship. We huddle up around the coach, he shares a few words of inspiration and then announces the shooter line-up.

"Natalie, you will be our fifth shooter, bring it home for us," he looks me in the eye and dips his chin. I return the eye contact and nod.

My pulse quickens and my legs ache. Four shooters for each team take their shots and we are still tied. I am the last to go. It is up to me.

I take a deep breath, exit the center circle and step decisively towards the penalty spot. My teammates are yelling "you got this," parents are cheering from the sidelines, and the opponent is staring a hole through the number five on my back. With each step I drown out the commotion and my vision narrows. It is only me, the ball, and the goal.

It's moments like these, that prepared me to perform in high-pressure environments, and to lead when everything is on the line. These moments, on the field, shaped me into the leader I am today and opened doors I never knew existed.

I can tell you right now, if someone would have told this rambunctious, brown-eyed girl from Texas that one day she would be a contributing author in a best-selling book series—with other women she admired—on a topic that fueled her soul, she wouldn't have believed it! Not for one second. But here I am doing just that.

Becoming an athlete was the moment I realized how much leadership mattered. At the time, I did not know this decision would change the trajectory of my life, but now I can see that it did.

When I was eight, I registered to play soccer, a sport I knew diddly squat about, for the deeply meaningful reason of spending more time with my best friend, Lisa. Unfortunately, the Field Mice had a full roster, and I was placed on the Cubs squad. The Cubs were made up of complete strangers and no Lisa. Even though I was disappointed I did not back out or wait for the next season.

This decision exposed me to a multitude of real-life adult situations. Such as being the new player on a well-established team, not knowing anyone, and having to build new skills while building new relationships. Sound familiar? How about your first day at work for your new job? Exciting and terrifying at the same time. Choosing to become an athlete also taught me innumerable life and leadership lessons.

The first lesson was the importance of supportive teammates and the impact of negative ones. Another one was realizing the power of a strong coach (leader) and the detriment to a team with a poor one. And regardless of your tenure, skill level, or position you can lead from any place on the field or within an organization. It's these powerful lessons learned while playing soccer through my adolescence that prepared me to play at the collegiate level.

As the only incoming female on the team to receive a full scholarship, I knew the responsibility I had to my team and to my academics, a balance I came to deploy in leadership roles in a corporate environment. While earning scholastic honors and awards for individual contributions, I was most proud of being selected as captain by my teammates and coaches for consecutive years. Being recognized as a leader amongst my peers and coaching staff was the greatest honor. Being the captain was a privilege and a responsibility I took wholeheartedly, and utilized the same approach to leading teams in my career. It was these experiences on and off the field that gave me the confidence and courage post-graduation to pursue a career in the healthcare industry.

That choice led to a successful nineteen-plus year career working in a range of organization types within the pharmaceutical and biotechnology industries. During these two decades, I've learned some key lessons in leadership.

Some lessons I learned the hard way, and maybe by sharing my experiences you can avoid them. At speaking engagements, I am often asked, "If you could go back to the start of your career and give yourself a piece of advice, what would it be?" The answer sounds simple now but took me years to understand—keep *your head up, your eyes open, and your heart centered*.

These three principals were learned as an athlete and applied throughout my career. This mentality heavily influenced my leadership philosophy. Leadership is not about the title you hold; it is about focusing on two key components—the people and the business. You cannot have one without the other; and if you choose to lead by only focusing on the business, your experience will be short-lived and lonely.

Focus for the business. It is imperative that you orient yourself, your team members, and the department within the organization. It is essential for you to know your role, where the role fits on the team, and the roles the other team members play—just like in soccer. And you must understand the role of the department and the department's place within the organization. If there are any gaps of knowledge in these areas—educate and advocate for yourself to fill them. Keeping your head up and your eyes open is the same when running down the field. It allows you to see the whole field, all the players, and new plays developing.

Focus for the People. At any age stage of your career, you can lead and influence those around you. Great leaders choose to make a positive impact, to bring out the best in others, to lead by example, and importantly to offer support and to encourage those who don't see their own talent. I was lucky to have a coach to recognize and encourage the natural talent I possessed in my early years of playing soccer and who taught me to play with my head up, eyes open, and to stay in-line with my core beliefs.

KEEP YOUR HEAD UP

After working at one of the world's largest healthcare companies with over 100,000 employees that had a philosophy of "if it ain't broke don't fix it" and then transitioning to a start-up company with under one hundred employees was jarring. In the start-up, speed, efficiency, creativity, and self-directed problem solving were treasured over the status quo of anything. Organizational agility was imperative.

I had to identify risks and opportunities, then align and integrate cross-functional resources into cohesive ad hoc teams to address and resolve the issues as quickly as possible. This approach needs a skillset that is sometimes over-flexed in a debilitating way in a start-up environment. At times when everything moves at lightning speed it is easy to miss the most obvious signs of trouble. It is imperative to slow down, observe what's changed, and scan your surroundings and the people around you. Head up.

You might be screaming at me saying, "That's insane, there's no slowing down in a start-up!" I don't mean careening to a stop, but I do mean finding a way to run without running blind. It is taking a Sunday drive while still needing to arrive at the destination by a certain time using the fastest, most efficient route possible. This is the balance: taking a leisurely, non-panicked approach, while being effective and focused on problem solving and arriving at the destination.

Keeping your head up also allows you to focus on possibilities with curiosity and awareness. Carving out time for forward thinking and building proactive plans vs. reactive ones is crucial. This approach allows us to question things, to welcome outside influences, and consider all possibilities. Jim Lovell says, "There are people who make things happen, there are people who watch things happen, and there are people who wonder what happened. To be successful, you need to be a person who makes things happen." You can only make things happen if you understand what needs to happen, which comes from knowing the entire landscape. Head up.

Great leaders in a fast-paced environment are the "clutch" of their teams and their organizations. Professor Linda Hill, the Wallace Brett Donham Professor of Business Administration at Harvard Business School, and coauthor, with Kent Lineback, of *Being the Boss: The 3 Imperatives for Becoming a Great Leader*, and author of *Becoming a Manager: How New Managers Master the Challenges of Leadership* tells us, *"To build a group that can navigate between the two speeds of the present and future."* A mistake often made is to stay head down grinding in the present; then before you know it, the future has arrived, and you are left behind.

Lesson Learned:
Being in the pharmaceutical industry for ten years I had heard glory stories of joining a start-up which had immense success and the subsequent prosperity it brought to its patients and employees on transaction day (the day when the company gets bought or goes IPO and the employees get a long awaited pay out). When presented the opportunity to join a start-up, where the CEO was an actual patient, I thought—this is my goal to score, so I took the shot.

Early on it was all about impact. I saw it as a huge opportunity to prove myself and create success like I had never experienced before. Well, I did just that. I was quickly promoted to a regional role, next the associate leader, then became the national leader for that function— then pow! I hit the ceiling--not of the organization but of the business unit I led.

The long, exhausting days turned into months which transformed into years, and when I finally lifted my head, it was too late. The organization had made acquisitions, had far different strategic plans, and I was pigeonholed to the one area of expertise I specialized in. In the end, I was sunsetted with the medicines I launched and supported for over a decade when their patent life expired.

Hindsight is 20/20 and I see now that if I had followed the principle of keeping my head up, I would not have been left out of future strategic plans. In fact, I would have been one of the architects creating the plan.

KEEP YOUR EYES OPEN

When you allow yourself to slow down, look up, and take in the world around you, your view invariably expands, revealing new paths and opportunities that might have remained hidden otherwise. Evaluate the organization from a drone's perspective. I learned this concept during my time at Harvard Business School where I was selected to participate in an Enterprise Leadership course.

Ranjay Gulati, Professor at Harvard Business School, best-selling author of *Deep Purpose*, and organizations and leadership expert, during a lecture, emphasized the importance of having an enterprise mindset and becoming an enterprise leader. He encouraged us to think differently through a broader and clearer perspective, to build authentic relationships which allow leaders to relate differently, to act differently, and demonstrate a true owner mindset. Had I learned about this mindset earlier in my career, I may have had a different experience at the start-up company.

Another benefit of keeping your eyes open is that it allows you to better understand the organizational inertia. As Ranjay Gulati puts it, "Culture is about the invisible rules." If you do not understand how your organization works, it becomes a game of "us vs. them." This is a battle no individual or individual's team will ever win. Discover who the creators of the cultural blueprint are and learn their vision, their aspirations, and the "why" behind their designated corporate pillars. Once you have that foundation, work to identify the necessary balance between leading your team and integrating them into the organization. Eyes Open.

Lesson Learned:
At that Havard training session, I was asked to identify the most influential advocates within my internal and

external networks, and I realized I was now: "Natalie, party of 3, your table is now ready."

Before I knew it, I was sitting alone at my table and my two dinner mates were ushered out the door. This is not a position a senior leader with ten years of experience at a single organization should find themselves in. If you're thinking this was a lonely and scary table to be seated at, you would be correct.

That is when I knew I too would soon be seeking excellence elsewhere. As you see, it's not always about your positive contribution to the organization or the perfect scores on your annual leadership surveys, there is so much more than that and it is imperative you are aware of it. *Eyes open* includes understanding the culture and the direction of the organization. For me, not having built and exercised my influence and network for a broader reach had grave consequences for my future within that organization. I didn't keep my eyes open.

KEEP YOUR HEART CENTERED

As you keep your head up, your eyes open, and passionately lead your people, you must protect yourself and your beliefs. Effective leadership requires an emotional connection to yourself and your team members. By saying *heart centered* I mean having the wisdom, courage, and compassion to lead others with authenticity, transparency, humility, and service. However, keeping centered is as challenging as it is beneficial. This central location protects you from—well, you! When your heart is located anywhere else, it exposes you to a multitude of vulnerabilities.

I am not a fan of roller coasters and accordingly I disdain the range of emotions experienced by the highs of leading a high performing team to the lows of being hurt by working with inauthentic colleagues. The lows sting, but they do not define you or symbolize that you are doing something wrong. In fact, it might be the opposite.

"New research demonstrates that performing at high levels can also come with some heavy costs: It can make our peers resent us and try to undermine our good work. This hypothesis might sound far-fetched, but it's actually common for peers to punish top performers. Decades of research on social comparisons show that when we size ourselves up relative to people who are better than we are (or as good as we are) on a particular dimension, we are likely to experience discomfort, envy, or fear. These emotions, in turn, affect our decisions and our interactions with others." (The

Problem with Being a Top Performer. *Scientific American, Fancesca Gino, July 5, 2017.*)

While these types of occurrences are unfortunate and out of our control, it's paramount we stay focused on what we can control, which is the unwavering commitment to putting people first. Get to know everyone on the team and partner with them in a purposeful way. This is not a one-time exercise; it must be consistently applied to build a foundation of trust.

Each relationship is curated and tailored to the needs of the individual. When instituting unity, make it your mission to create an unbreakable team bond with a group of individuals who may not like each other, know each other, or want to engage in teamwork authentically. Just like on the soccer field, a shared purpose creates a foundation of aligned commitment, helping team members achieve their individual potential and the team achieve shared success. "The strength of the team is each individual member. The strength of each member is the team." —Phil Jackson

Lesson Learned:
Throughout the life of my career, I have had immense success connecting with people on a deep level, gifting

me some of the most cherished relationships I possess today. Authenticity and transparency are in my DNA. Those who meet me know I care about *who* they are, *what* they have to say, and *how* I can support them. It never was, or will ever be, about what they can do for me or who they know.

Dr. Nicholas A. Pearce, an award-winning Clinical Professor of Management & Organizations at the Northwestern University Kellogg School of Management and author of the bestselling book, *The Purpose Path: A Guide to Pursuing Your Authentic Life's Work*, deep dives into the importance of creating your personal scorecard for success: "... knowing your own values and then allowing those values to guide what success means to and for you—and only you."

When creating a personal scorecard for success in leadership, I tapped into the invaluable lessons learned as an athlete, what not to do from my worst managers and coaches and what to do from the best ones. This self-created scorecard gave me the power to know if I am attaining the goals set for me—by me. There is no one person or one situation that can strip me of achieving my defined success. This is a powerful gift of leading with your heart center that I recommend you create for yourself.

Get started with your scorecard by answering the

question, "What does true success mean *to* and *for* you?" An important thought Professor Pearce left the group to ponder and one I will leave with you is, "When it is all said and done, and you find out that the ladder you've been climbing all those years was leaning on the wrong wall, what do you do when you realize you've hit the top but are left unfilled?" (The Purpose Path: A Guide to Pursuing Your Authentic Life's Work) You have the power to define what true success as a leader is to you and how you want to achieve it.

This little girl from Texas' story isn't over yet and neither is yours! As a new Italian resident, I am embarking on my next aspiration of applying this learning and personal philosophy on leadership to a global market. I not only hope to inspire more female leaders but to celebrate our allies and mentors helping each organization achieve new heights without compromising the values of their employees and partnerships.

As the noise faded away, I placed the ball on the penalty mark and took the shot. The sound of the ball hitting the back of the net is equally as memorable as winning the championship. However, it is not whether the shot went in or not, it's that I had the courage to take it and carry the responsibility of the outcome. That is leadership.

Leaders must be accountable and carry the weight of wins and losses. Be confident in who you are and your ability to positively impact those around you no matter where you sit in the organization.

Lace up your cleats. Take the field. Keep your head up, eyes open, and heart centered.

INTRODUCING
JENNIFER PESTIKAS

Jennifer Pestikas, MBA, CPC, ELI-MP, is an executive, podcaster, career and leadership coach, and best-selling author. Jennifer has over twenty years' experience in the financial services industry and is currently the Senior Vice President of Business Development of a Chicagoland financial institution. Jennifer understands the necessary skills to make significant leaps in your career, including mindset, asking for what you want, interviewing skills, the ability to negotiate, executive presence and more.

In addition to her corporate work, Jennifer is now leveraging her experience with her personal company, Brave Women at Work. She helps her clients better identify their strengths, what they want, what is holding them back and how to remove these barriers so they can take bolder and braver action in their careers.

Jennifer has a Bachelors in French and Spanish from

Indiana University and an M.B.A. from Lake Forest Graduate School of Management. She is also a Certified Professional Coach and an Energy Leadership Index (ELI) Master Practitioner from the Institute for Professional Excellence in Coaching (IPEC).

You can find Jennifer online at bravewomenatwork. com. Please also connect with Jennifer on LinkedIn or listen to her podcast, Brave Women at Work, which is available on all major podcast platforms. You can also pick up a copy of Jennifer's other books, Brave Women at Work: Stories of Resilience and Brave Women at Work: Lessons in Confidence, which are anthologies of women's real-life stories of overcoming professional and personal challenges.

Outside of work, Jennifer loves spending time with her husband and two daughters, reading, going to the movies, and taking travel adventures with her family.

DECISIONS, DECISIONS, DECISIONS

"Be willing to make decisions. That's the most important quality in a good leader."
—George S. Patton Jr.

What are the qualities of a good leader? A simple Google search results in 20 million websites or pages to learn what a good leader is. Twenty million! There is tons of interest and hot debate on what qualities separate a good leader from a bad one. I have had a range of leadership experiences in my twenty-plus years in corporate America. Throughout my career, there have been key decisions and inflexion points that I had to either shrink from or step into and lead through. It's in these seemingly small decisions that we hone our leadership skills and develop our leadership style. I share with you a selection of decisions, what I've learned from them, and their long-lasting impacts on my career and life.

DECISION #1: THE LONG JOURNEY TO FRIENDSHIP

"You don't have to fly out here to let me go," Ben said.

Ben, a financial advisor, and a fully commissioned salesperson on my team, was underperforming and had low sales numbers. We couldn't afford to keep an under-performer on staff for long. Importantly, keeping Ben on the team would negatively impact morale.

"Of course, I need to come out to see you for this meeting. It is not right to do this in a phone call," I said, releasing the breath I didn't realize I was holding. I knew that Ben was trying to get the termination over with, protect his dignity, save me the trip, and make the process easier for both of us; but to me it mattered to do it face-to-face. I didn't feel right terminating his position over the phone and I booked a ticket to Seattle.

After the long flight, as luck would have it, I was assigned a sports car for my rental. I always wanted to drive a Ford Mustang and here was my chance. I raced down the highway, with the windows down and Pearl Jam blaring on the radio. The Seattle clouds parted, and the sun warmed my face and lifted my spirits. I belted out the lyrics to *Even Flow* and imagined I was on vacation instead of about to change someone's life and eliminate their job.

I inched along in the Seattle traffic and got closer to Ben's office. My heart rate increased, my palms were clammy, and I gripped the steering wheel a bit tighter. I've never been good at terminating employees. I know it is business, but it is difficult to separate business from the person, even when it is the right thing to do for the organization. My Human Resource colleague said to me months earlier, "If terminating employees no longer fazes you, then there's probably something wrong. It never gets easier." My colleague's statement floated across my brain and comforted me as I pulled into the parking lot. I wasn't weak as a leader. I was a leader experiencing a human moment.

I strolled through the lobby of the branch and greeted Ben in his office. He was already packing up since he knew this moment was coming. I asked him to sit down so we could talk. My voice quavered, but I remained steadfast during the conversation. I explained why this action had to be taken, specifically the poor performance and low sales production. He indicated agreement and understanding; he signed the paperwork, and it was over.

So, what did I do next? Did I leave Ben's office and escape to the fast car, sunshine, and loud music? Nope. At that moment, I decided to help pack and load boxes into his car. I was a leader experiencing a human moment with Ben. Even though his employment at our company was about to end, it didn't make him or me less human. Ben deserved respect and was willing to accept my help. As we packed up the last of his boxes, we talked idly about his next steps, and I wished him well. As I climbed back into the Mustang, I didn't think I would ever see Ben again.

I was wrong. Two years later at a different banking institution and as a VP of Marketing, I received a call from Amy, a Seattle-based investment assistant that I had become friends with while in my last role. She happily told me that she had been dating someone for the last year and that I knew the person. I was confused. How could I possibly know the person? I don't know anyone in Seattle.

"Who are you dating, Amy?" I inquired.

"Well—it's Ben," she paused.

My breath caught in my chest and time stood still. "Are you kidding me?"

"No, I am not kidding," she said. "Ben and I are in a pretty serious relationship." My head was spinning. I was so stunned; I couldn't believe it. "Amy, do you know that I had to let Ben go from the last company we worked at?" I mewled.

"Of course! Ben told me all about it," she laughed.

"Does he hate me and never want to speak to me again?"

"God, no. You have it all wrong. Ben thinks it is one of the classiest things he has ever had a manager do. You didn't have to come all the way here to have the conversation, but you did. It was a win for everyone because now he is at a job that is a better fit and he loves it."

There it was: confirmation that my decision to fly from Chicago to Seattle to talk with him face-to-face was the right one. By doing right by him even in the difficult moment, it propelled him forward. Ben ended up as a successful financial advisor and asset manager for a large investment firm. Then he became the primary owner and partner of that same business. The termination did not negatively impact his life; it was done professionally, and he went on to even greater success.

Ben and Amy got married and guess who received a wedding invitation? When I opened it, I laughed out loud until my stomach ached. I was the last person I thought they would invite, but there I was, faced with another decision. Should I stay home? Or fly across the country and go?

After checking in with myself, I knew in my heart what I would do. I flew to Seattle to attend and celebrate their wedding. As I flew across the country, I smiled, relieved that I was making the trip under different circumstances, but this time my rental car was not nearly as cool—a Chevy Malibu. I relish the fact that what started out as a tough leadership decision ended up in a life-long friendship.

So, what did I learn in this situation? I learned that leaders are human too. I am human. There are times when making a tough decision, like flying across the country for a termination, is the right thing to do. And instead of simply focusing on the task, look beyond it and check in with your employee to see what they need. Finally, it is imperative not to ruin relationships. You never know where your life and career will take you. Maybe someone you managed in a prior company may end up as a colleague or a future boss. Maybe you will manage that person in a different capacity down the road. Or maybe, just maybe, you will end up at that person's wedding.

DECISION #2: LEANING IN

"Sheryl Sandberg?" I questioned. "Who is Sheryl Sandberg?"

I was about to find out. It was 2013, and I was in San Francisco at a huge conference that took over the city. Attending a conference with over 150,000 people was overwhelming. Everywhere, I went, there was a sea of people crowding me, entering my personal space. The technology and content went way over my head and took all my attention to grasp. The vastness of the conference space was boggling. By the third day, my eyes glazed over, and my brain shut down. It was too much. I chalked the experience up as a waste of time, felt disappointed, and planned my early escape.

I was about to leave when a stranger asked if I was going to attend the keynote speech by Sheryl Sandberg.

"Who is Sheryl Sandberg?" I asked.

"She is the COO of Facebook (now Meta)," the fellow conference goer said. "She has a new book out. It's called *Lean In*."

"Maybe I'll check it out," I quipped, not sure if I would go or not.

Even though I waffled, I thought *why not*, and made my way to the keynote speech. The monstrous hotel ballroom had hundreds of seats and there was a hardcover copy of *Lean In* placed neatly on each chair throughout the entire room. I found a seat, picked up the book, and flipped through it. It looked like good reading for the flight home.

With the ballroom full, Sheryl entered the stage with visible energy, confidence, and inspiration. I was awestruck and totally enamored. She talked about "leaning into our careers" and that "we could have it all." We didn't need to select motherhood or a career. We didn't have to lean into family at the expense of our advancement.

Sheryl was the pastor, and I was the religious devotee. It felt like she was speaking directly to me, saying exactly what I needed to hear. I drank the "women can do it all" Kool-Aid, and I couldn't wait to read the book.

I boarded the plane and rushed to my seat and immediately started reading *Lean In*. After that, I can't tell you what happened. I was transported into the world she created for female leaders. The next four hours were a blur of words and page turning. I devoured the book and all the concepts within it.

As the plane started its descent towards O'Hare, I consumed the last pages and alit with motivation. I learned about *Lean In* circles, women's only groups that foster leadership and the proliferation of the principles covered in the book. As we taxied to the gate, I decided to write a recommendation and pitch the idea to my boss, the CEO, for a *Lean In* circle. My company needed a *Lean In* circle, and I was the person that was going to lead it.

A few weeks later, I presented the recommendation to my boss. My body was vibrating with excitement; I was so thrilled with this idea and opportunity. I am an entrepreneur at heart and love improvement and growth in all forms and facets. When I delivered the recommendation to my boss, he became quiet and contemplative.

My heart sank and I worried, *what if he declines my*

idea to start a Lean In circle? Only now did I think he might decline my proposal; I was blind with ambition and did not think he would say anything but *Yes!* The clock ticked on the wall behind him, and the second hand was in slow motion. I *leaned into* the silence and gave him space to consider.

"Jen, I like the idea, but I would like you to broaden it to include all leaders in the organization, both female and male. By launching a leadership group like this, it will set our organization apart."

"Ah," I paused to collect my thoughts. "Let me consider this further."

I didn't anticipate this response. While he wasn't giving me an easy yes, he also wasn't saying no. Instead of getting angry at him for missing the point that women need a space for leadership development, I worked on the problem.

Here was another choice. Would I dig my heels and hold fast to the original idea? Or would I be willing to pivot away from my first recommendation into something that would be approved? I made the pivot because I wanted to make it happen regardless. Ultimately, I could still create the space for learning and development I yearned for. I adjusted the recommendation to have it as a co-ed opportunity and sent the revision to my boss via email.

The next day, my boss came into my office with a copy of my recommendation with additional changes. I completed another round of revisions. My boss then asked me to present that version to my colleagues in the management team. More commentary and changes from the group followed.

It took me nine months to get final approval on the leadership group. I could have given up: the original idea had taken a whole new shape, but with some of the same foundational elements. I did not give up. I learned that patience and persistence, combined with a willingness to adjust my original vision, pays off. One year after I presented the idea to my boss, the leadership group at my organization, for all employees—both female and male—was born.

Since the leadership group started in 2014, over thirty percent of employees in the organization have participated in the group and it continues 'til today. The participants represent all departments across the company and range from entry-level employees to senior management. The group has also been expanded to include three levels of leadership that focus on different areas. Leadership 1.0 focuses on the idea of "why" with the book *Start with Why* by Simon Sinek; Leadership 2.0 focuses on inspiration; and Leadership 3.0 focuses on innovation. The creation of this group has helped me become a better leader and is a highlight of my career.

The original idea, ignited as I sat in the enormous ballroom in San Francisco—which luckily, I chose to attend—became a much broader opportunity for the organization, and me. Admittedly, it did morph well beyond developing women in leadership and ensuring that they *lean in*. This solution is what was needed for the organization at that time, but I never let go of that initial passion. Women deserve their own space to develop and lead, and thus Brave Women at Work was launched. Brave Women at Work, all the offerings and materials, serve the purpose of creating a space to lead, develop, and celebrate women.

DECISION #3: STICKING TO MY GUNS

"We need to make a change," I announced.

The conference room fell silent, and the strategic planning session screeched to a halt.

This was not a popular or even sexy idea. No one wanted to make a large digital system change. It is tedious, scary, and rife with the possibility of failure and delays. Customers and employees are rarely fans of big digital infrastructure changes.

"We need to make the change," I stated again,

attempting to generate a response from anyone. I looked at the CEO and each of my colleagues.

"I am not convinced yet that we do," the CEO replied. "We do not change for change's sake."

I was exasperated. After three years of research, internally scheduled demonstrations, and discussions with third-party referrals, the executive team was still not convinced we needed to change our digital services system to improve the customer experience. I tried not to take this rejection personally, even though it was hard not to. I hung onto the CEO's word "yet" and wondered if I should let this go or stick to my guns. I took a jagged breath in and secured an inner calm.

"What do you need to see to take this from *not yet* to *yes* to make this change?"

"I am not sure," he glanced up to me with a small smile. "Yet."

I dug in. We needed this change, I knew it. Three years of research emboldened me with that knowledge. I had to do whatever it took to get the executive team to understand the critical need for this update. Not because *I* needed to be right, but because it *was* the right change for the organization and our customers. Without this the customer experience and the infrastructure would not be in line with the competition.

I dove deeper into the research. I challenged the vendors to distill technical jargon into something executives understood. I asked tough questions and requested their attendance with the executive team. I reviewed my references, asked more questions, even recording several of the conversations for my own and the executives' references as needed. My colleagues thought I was nuts and going way beyond what was necessary. It was a big decision for the leadership team and an even bigger change for the organization. I could not leave any compelling information out.

Years of effort paid off. During a vendor discussion, I asked about development and investments into our current digital platform. The representative from the vendor admitted that the investments were being siphoned off and would likely cease in the coming years; only maintenance and support would be offered. This was critical information to bolster the change recommendation.

Sure, our current platform was passable, but we needed to invest in the change now for a superior customer experience and because the investment and development of the current platform was ending. I pitched it again with this new information and watched my CEO's face as his decision transformed from *not convinced yet* to *this is a serious possibility.*

The CEO took the next action, ensuring that the executive team knew the status of the platform and what needed to change. Comprehensive conversations on options, risks, and the level of change management required to support such a change were held. Seeing the engagement and discussion around the table, I knew I made the right decision to stick to my guns, do the work it took to ensure our business was competitive, and to select a platform upon which our business would thrive. My three-years-plus of effort was coming to fruition, even when I doubted myself and my colleagues said it wasn't worth it.

Do you want to know the kicker? While I was proud that I secured the CEO's buy-in to change the organization's digital platform, the CEO didn't end up going forward with my preferred vendor selection. Again, I faced a decision. Should I get angry that the company didn't select the vendor I had my heart set on? For a while, I did just that.

I was frustrated. After all, it had been three years of hard work. I was having another human moment. After a few weeks of frustration, I decided to let it go. As they say, "Sometimes them's the breaks." I accepted that, while I could celebrate the win that the organization would make a digital change, I was ultimately not responsible for the final vendor decision. Was that difficult? Heck yes. Was it necessary? Also, yes.

THE LEARNINGS

Leadership is filled with moments of decisions; some seem large, and some seem small. It's in these decisions that you develop your leadership muscle and become the leader you were meant to be.

Vince Lombardi told us, "Leaders are not born. They are made." These decisions once made helped shape my leadership approach and who I am as a human and leader. Certainly, there are a ton of decisions I made without so rosy consequences, but those too are formative—sometimes we learn what *not* to do.

All these critical decisive moments taught me to manage the total person, not just the task. They taught me about doing the right thing no matter what, even if it is inconvenient, unexpected, or even unnecessary. They taught me about following your passion, ideas, being flexible, and willing to collaborate to create a different and new outcome. And they taught me to listen to my intuition, stick to my guns, and be tenacious in seeing something through, even when it is challenging or unpopular.

I am a powerful leader. I love developing, caring for, and helping people achieve their dreams through my approach to leadership.

INTRODUCING
RONICKA BRISCOE

Ronicka Harrison Briscoe is a proud New Orleans native and first-generation college graduate. In 2006, she was graduated cum laude from Xavier University of Louisiana in New Orleans, where she earned a Bachelor of Arts degree in political science with a minor in environmental studies with a focus on environmental justice.

Ronicka is an interdisciplinary scholar who has formally studied political science, public administration (non-profit management), business, and executive leadership with an emphasis on the lived experiences of Black women in leadership. She has spent her career in education as a teacher, administrator, educational consultant, and strategist. Ronicka has worked at every level of the education system (early childhood through 12 grade and university); in a variety of types of institutions (traditional, charter, private, etc.) and regions (urban, suburban, and rural); specializing in organizational strategy, executive leadership, community engagement, and culturally responsive and equitable classrooms.

Ronicka co-founded Legacy Foundation for Girls in 2018, a 501(c)3 organization whose mission is to educate, encourage and empower girls and young mothers of color to be a catalyst for change through transformational programs. She is actively involved in promoting positive and sustainable community change through board service in the following organizations: 826 New Orleans (Immediate Past President); 826 National; Parent Leadership Training Institute—Civic Design Team; and Teach for America—Alumni Advisory (Co-Chair).

Ronicka completed requirements for the Doctor of Philosophy degree in the fall of 2021 in executive leadership at the University of Holy Cross, New Orleans, resulting in her making university history, becoming the first student to earn a Ph.D. in the program.

Ronicka has continued to consult nationally as an educational strategist. She travels the country as a speaker, panelist, and coalition builder.

Ronicka is grateful for the support of her mother and sister. She is happily married and has two beautiful children.

WINNING ON THE ROAD

Winning on the road is an achievement. The visiting team travels to unknown environments to compete against a home team. The trip is typically long and arduous, making it more difficult for fans to attend. The trek may involve changing time zones and competing in unfamiliar climates. The visiting team is welcomed with basic amenities and locker rooms that reek, reminding players that they are no longer in the comfort of their home facilities. When the visiting team walks onto the court or field, the roaring by the home team fans is inescapable. The view from the bench on the visiting side ensures the home team spirit is on full display: fans dressed in team paraphernalia, large signs, and loud cheering. Heckling from the stands can be resounding and hostile. Each glance at the scoreboard is a reminder that there is a home team and a visiting team. The atmosphere is intimidating for even the fiercest visiting competitors, requiring both mental and physical preparedness to compete.

For the visiting team, the pressure is immense for the best players to step up, perform, and keep the team motivated. Under the conditions described, achieving victory on the road is no easy feat. Yet, it may be one of the most indisputable indicators of undeniable talent, toughness, and tenacity when accomplished. The win is much sweeter when clenched on the road!

Winning on the Road is a powerful metaphor I coined to capture the unique challenges and experiences that women, especially Women of Color and Black women, encounter as they strive to advance in their professional careers and reach leadership positions. This metaphor implies that the journey to success for women leaders is comparable to the challenges women athletes encounter as they fight to achieve success in the face of adversity and systemic barriers that require the highest levels of resilience, determination, and the ability to persevere. *Winning on the Road* describes the additional challenges and complexities faced by women from historically marginalized backgrounds in the workplace, such as discrimination, bias, and lack of representation. *Winning on the Road* emphasizes the importance of acknowledging and addressing these challenges to create a more equitable and inclusive environment where all women have the opportunity to succeed.

I developed this metaphor during research for my doctoral dissertation as I set out to understand what Black women, who beat the odds to attain top level leadership positions, attribute to their success. I knew if I learned more about the approaches these successful women used to reach their position and the strategies employed to navigate their professional careers and overcome obstacles, the findings would be a powerful gift to myself; and I could then share it with the next generation of women leaders.

I interviewed Black women across the country, in various professions, that ranged from education, business, legal, to public service. Each of their stories was unique, but a clear and undeniable pattern emerged. They each had to *win on the road* and in most cases on the road was inside the organization that recruited and placed them.

In this chapter, I introduce profiles of Black women athletes who successfully demonstrated what it took to *win on the road* and how their experiences parallel those Black women who serve in executive leadership positions. I share the key findings and action steps. If you are an early career professional, the insights assist your strategic planning and your ascension into leadership. If you are an experienced leader, there are nuggets you can consider as you enter the next phase of your career.

SERENA WILLIAMS, GREATNESS PERSONIFIED AND GREATNESS DEHUMANIZED

Serena and her sister Venus entered the white-dominated field of professional tennis as teenagers hailing from Compton, California, known as one of the roughest urban areas in America. While their counterparts learned to play in resorts, country clubs, tennis academies, and associations, the Williams sisters learned to play in neighborhood parks. They entered tennis with their father at their side, their biggest fan and most strident coach. When they stepped onto the court, they did so with their natural hair tightly braided with traditional African beads on the end. Immediately, their presence created negative commentary.

As Venus and Serena played with high energy and intensity, their braids loosened, and the beads would fall to the court, resulting in fines on more than one occasion. As time progressed, the mainstream media routinely compared Serena's physical appearance, dark brown skin, and muscular build to monkeys and gorillas. Serena's femininity was criticized by members of the professional tennis community. Her athletic physique led commentators to allege Serena's extraordinary talent was unnatural and was somehow an unfair advantage. Chris Evert, a former female professional tennis player, is quoted as saying, "[Serena's] athletic ability and raw aggression makes it hard for the women who aren't Amazons to compete." Records show that Serena experienced more random drug tests than any other professional tennis player. (Deadspin, Laura Wagner, June 27, 2018)

Serena routinely received as much media attention about the outfits she chose to wear during competitions as the titles she won. Serena was seen on the court wearing bright colors, tutus, and even an all-black compression pantsuit. In 2018, Nike designed a special compression suit for Serena to ensure adequate blood flow during her matches after she suffered illness due to blood clots. The French Tennis Federation labeled the compression suit a "catsuit" as intimidating and they issued a new sanction restricting such attire. Nike responded to the newly imposed rule with a social media post featuring Serena in the compression suit along with the following caption: "You can take the superhero out of her costume, but you can never take her superpowers. #justdoit." Although this may appear to be an isolated incident, changing the rules of the game is not a new phenomenon for Black athletes, particularly women. The bodies of Black women are over-policed, and psychological harm is inflicted through absurd rules intentionally crafted to penalize and dehumanize.

Despite Serena's lived experiences, she has beaten the odds and dominated the world of tennis. Serena won twenty-three Grand Slam singles titles, the most of any tennis player in Open Era tennis, male or female, Black or white. She won thirty-nine Grand Slam titles and achieved Olympic greatness by earning four gold medals. The impeccable resume Serena amassed should be enough to level the playing field and eliminate racism and sexism in the sport. And yet, the lived experiences of Serena prove that the intersection of race and gender shapes the multifaceted experiences Black women have in the workplace.

In 2019, one year after the controversial U.S. Open match between Serena and Naomi Osaka, Serena penned an open letter in *BAZAAR* magazine. In the letter, Serena discusses the incident. During the 2018 U.S. Open, Serena was issued three violations for comments she made to the umpire. The umpire accused Serena of having coaching interactions during the match, which is against the rules. Serena vehemently denies being coached during the game by stating, "I don't cheat to win. I'd rather lose." She demanded an apology from the umpire, which led to the third violation. The three violations resulted in a loss for Serena and a first Grand Slam victory for Naomi. The momentous occasion was stolen from Naomi by the commentary surrounding the match and Serena's inter-actions with the umpire. Serena found herself pleading to the world to let Naomi have her moment while she attempted to internally reconcile the inequitable factors that led to her opportunity for victory to be taken away. Serena describes her feelings by stating, "I felt defeated and disrespected by a sport that I love—one that I had dedicated my life to and that my family truly changed, not because we were welcomed, but because we wouldn't stop winning." (Sports Illustrated, Emily Caron, July 9, 2019)

Often, representation by a Black person in a white-dominated field or environment is misunderstood as integration and somehow representative of an anti-rac-ist environment. Similarly, if a woman is present in a male-dominated arena, her presence is misinterpreted as gender equity rather than professional competence. However, the reality is the opposite because they are at the intersection of a marginalized racial and gender identity converging with forms of oppression in the workplace.

Serena and other Black women athletes are often told to leave it all on the field or shut up and play; however, the disrespect, disregard, and discrimination are difficult to ignore, and quite frankly should not be ignored. Serena makes the claim that, "This incident, though excruciating for us to endure, exemplified how thousands of women in every area of the workforce are treated every day."

SIMONE BILES, THE GOAT

Gymnastics is a sport that requires athletes to compete as individuals and as a team, much like executive leadership. Although executive leaders are being evaluated on their individual performance, the overall performance of the team reflects the ability of the leader to develop and lead their team effectively.

Gymnastics requires mental and physical strength, precision, and discipline. Gymnasts spend countless hours practicing and perfecting their techniques with the dream of one day competing at the Olympic games. The requirements are similar for leaders who desire to lead at the highest level: mental and physical well-being, attention to detail, laser-like focus, and an unwavering commitment to the work. Unfortunately, only a few are afforded this honor and opportunity.

For Black women who aspire to compete as an Olympic gymnast or lead an organization as the president or chief executive officer (CEO), the chances are improbable based on historical accounts. The United

States first entered a gymnastics team of women during the 1963 Olympic games. It wasn't until 1992 that a Black woman gymnast would compete as a member of Team USA in the Olympics. Betty Okino earned a team bronze medal that year. Thirty years later, Simone Biles, standing at four feet eight inches tall with smooth mocha brown skin and a dazzling smile, found herself as arguably the greatest gymnast of all time. The acronym GOAT is often used to convey the greatest of all times. Simone often wears an image of a goat inconspicuously placed on her competition leotard in rhinestones to remind herself of her greatness.

In the 2016 Olympics, Simone won individual gold medals in the categories of all-around, vault, and floor and multiple team gold medals. Following these unprecedented victories, Simone was interviewed. During the interview, the commentator compared her to several male athletes who were considered unrivaled in their respective sports. She responded, "I am not the next Usain Bolt or Michael Phelps. I am the first Simone Biles." In this instance, the commentator compared the talent Simone possessed to white and Black male athletes in sports outside of gymnastics. The commentator attempted to deprive Simone of her rightful place at the top of the gymnastics charts for women, strip her of her femininity, and make a discordant comparison. In response, Simone demanded that the commentator see her as a woman, a Black woman, and a fierce athlete. She has charted her path to ascend to the highest level in gymnastics. She *is* the GOAT.

Currently ranked number one in the world, Simone successfully transformed traditional gymnastics moves and techniques and elevated the complexity to an unparalleled level. She mastered skills other gymnasts could not even attempt; her talent is unmatched even at the highest level in her sport. As a result of her superior talent, the International Gymnastics Federation imposed a rule that lowers the number of points a gymnast could receive for successfully executing such complex moves.

Simone is the singular gymnast capable of these difficult moves; one must conclude that the rules intentionally penalize her exceptional talent. Subsequently, the newly created guidelines attempt to stifle creativity, humble her expectations for scores, and serve as a mechanism to limit her achievement. After surviving a tumultuous childhood that included foster care and sexual abuse, Simone met the bar for excellence in gymnastics and ascended to the highest level in the sport. She double-somersaulted over the bar, only to find the people who controlled the bar changed the rules and diminish her achievements.

For many Black women in leadership, the experience of Simone was understood and personally experienced. As Black women vying for top-level roles in organizations, the path is often cluttered with challenges, hurdles, and newly imposed rules or policies to further disenfranchise, discourage, and disrupt their desires to reach the top. Even at the highest levels, Black women often experience limitations on what they are allowed to achieve. Black women are often harshly evaluated, and their work unfairly scrutinized; then when they succeed, the rules might change.

THE PLAYBOOK

While rooted in the experiences of Black Women Leaders across America, the seven recommendations within this playbook have transcended cultural confines, fostering connections that resonate universally. As I've shared this my findings and my thesis work nationwide, women from diverse backgrounds have found relatability and connectivity within its insights. Despite its origins, this research has proven to be a unifying force, bridging gaps, and speaking to the common experiences and aspirations shared by women across a spectrum of identities and life paths.

As I conducted research, a few meaningful and practical recommendations for Black women who desire to achieve executive leadership roles revealed themselves.

Understanding the lived experiences of Black women who are winning on the road and functioning in top positions in their companies proved to be instructive and informative. There are seven substantive recommendations that are a blueprint or playbook for aspiring leaders—concrete actions to take to build your own strategic plan to rise to the top.

While initially drawn from the lived experiences of Black Women Leaders across America, this research extends beyond cultural boundaries, fostering connections that resonate universally. As I've presented these insights nationwide, women from diverse backgrounds have discovered relatability and connectivity within its framework. From the experiences of Black women achieving executive leadership, seven substantive recommendations emerged, offering a practical blueprint for aspiring leaders. These recommendations, born from the journeys of successful Black women navigating top positions, offer a strategic playbook for rising to leadership roles. They encapsulate concrete actions to construct a personal strategic plan, providing guidance for individuals aspiring to ascend in their careers, regardless of their backgrounds or identities.

#1 —KNOCK IT OUT OF THE PARK

When baseball players knock it out of the park, they hit the ball so hard that it is no longer in the field of play, and the athlete scores. Knocking it out of the park is not easy, and those who accomplish it build a strong reputation.

Black women who have reached the highest levels of leadership, typically spend the early years of their professional careers building their expertise and reputations, essentially taking every opportunity to knock it out of the park.

Women often believe that working hard and doing a great job will get them recognition and promotions. The reality is that just as much work must be invested in building a notable reputation in the industry. Some of those ways include:

LINKEDIN PRESENCE

Celebrate your success on professional platforms like LinkedIn. Leverage the platform to tell your story of success on your own terms. Use the platform to connect with leaders in your industry and invite them to connect with you.

Throughout this year, I engaged in multiple conference presentations wherein I actively encouraged attendees to connect with me on LinkedIn, thereby expanding my professional network. Subsequently, following each event, I diligently shared photographs and succinct summaries of the sessions along with my personal reflections. I made it a point to tag individuals I encountered during these conferences, and I also extended invitations to my newly formed connections to tag me in their respective posts. This strategy provided my LinkedIn network with a firsthand view of the conferences and my presentations, offering them valuable insights into my expertise. As a result, it effectively established my niche within the industry, consequently leading to further opportunities for speaking engagements.

SACRIFICES OF SUCCESS

The flipside of pouring oneself into a professional career at an early age is the navigation of romantic relationships, marriage, starting a family and/or growing a family.

When speaking to college-aged young women, I am often asked how I navigate my career, marriage, and children. The reality is, it is not easy, and each person has to develop a path that works for them, and their family.

I stood in front of the entire school faculty, at the school's back-to-school professional development day. I spent all summer planning for it. I was in my third year as assistant principal and leader of academics. I was thirty years old, pregnant with my second child, a boy. I had gained twice the amount of weight during this pregnancy as I had during my first, and I looked and felt huge.

Although WJ was due on August 12th, I was determined

to get through the week of professional development. As I
spoke about classroom engagement, warm fluid slid down
my leg. "Um, I know I am not peeing, right now." I excused
myself and rushed to the bathroom. My water had broken in
front of the entire faculty.

I can laugh at that moment now, but when I really
think about it, I wonder why was I at work that day? I
was two weeks away from my due date. I should have
been at home waiting for my beautiful baby boy to arrive.
I was there because I was a young leader, I was good at
my job, and I did not want my pregnancy to slow down
my career or impact my performance. Today I am not
sure if I would change my decision but can say that I am
glad I opted for a long dress that day. I was committed
to knocking it out of the park no matter what my health
or condition.

I discovered the paramount importance of prioritizing both physical and mental well-being while pursuing
leadership at the highest levels. Here are some recommendations aimed at assisting you in proactively planning for
the physical and mental demands inherent in pursuing
leadership roles:

Create a life plan: Create a timeline that includes goals and
sets parameters. Include both personal and professional

milestones. Determine the sacrifices that will be necessary on the journey. Decide the path.

Maintain physical and mental health: Prioritize doctors' appointments and remain aware of changes to the body. Understand how everyday experiences impact overall health. If you think it may be a possibility to have children, consider freezing your eggs, so you can be prepared.

#2 —FIRST-ROUND DRAFT PICK

The goal of every talented college basketball and football player is to be chosen as a first-round draft pick. The individuals selected during the first round are the best of the best and are the top-performing athletes. The women I interviewed indicated that they too have been "drafted" to serve in their leadership role. Many of the women were recruited for their positions via a headhunter or an executive recruiter, while others were personally tapped by the CEO or other high-ranking leaders of the organization.

The ability of women to successfully build strong reputations in their sector led to them being actively pursued for executive leadership positions. Most of the women I interviewed did not blindly apply for their current roles. They were sought out and recruited.

The idea of women strategically building their

acumens and reputations by knocking it out of the park early in their careers appeared to have a strong connection to being a first-round draft pick. Most participants were first-round draft picks and were appointed to their roles based on their expertise and track records of success.

First-Round Draft Pick, but Treated Like a Walk-On

In less than a decade into my career and before turning 30, I became an assistant principal, driven by my ambition to secure my first Principalship. An opportunity emerged to take on a Principalship. Though I initially questioned my aspirations, the CEO's persistence and pressure continued. After several meetings and negotiations, I eventually secured the Principalship. However, less than six months into this role, a significant setback occurred—the CEO who recruited me passed away, leaving new leadership at the organization. This change drastically shifted the culture of the organization. As someone once highly recruited and valued, I now found myself facing micromanagement and a challenging environment under the new CEO's leadership, turning what was once a promising opportunity into a deeply challenging professional experience, moving from MVP treatment to Walk-On treatment very quickly.

#3 —DIVERSE TEAM OF TRAINERS

Athletic trainers are often charged with the responsibility of ensuring players are taking the proper precautions and are preventing injuries. Trainers evaluate the athletic abilities of their players and give critical advice. Every star athlete has a trainer. The most elite have a team of trainers. A parallel is drawn between the role of an athletic trainer and the role that mentors play in the lives of professional women. The women I interviewed were explicit in identifying mentorship from a diverse group of "trainers" as a key activity in their preparation for executive leadership. Generally, women believed in identifying a diverse group of mentors in gender, profession, experience, and ethnicity. Their mentorship experiences allowed for authentic relationships, building allyships, and learning from the trusted group of mentors. Each mentor played a unique role and brought a different perspective to the table regarding offering support.

Having trustworthy mentors who are both male and female, from various ethnic backgrounds, and who have a diverse spectrum of experiences is necessary to broaden the mentee's perspective and broaden their knowledge base. Research shows that Americans lack racial diversity in personal and professional networks. Additionally, those who cultivate racially homogeneous networks and have the most access to those in positions of power effectively create isolated networks that exclude outsiders. Intentionally connecting with racially diverse mentors and working toward widening networks is important for career advancement. Establish connections with a vast network of credible mentors and advisors. Leaders require great mentors who provide perspective, constructive comments, advice, and real support. It is critical to have a reliable thought partner. These people are essential in assisting the leader in developing an awareness of her leadership style and method and providing a framework and support system necessary for growth and development. The participants in my doctoral thesis work emphasized the importance of mentors being varied in gender, age, race, ethnicity, and experience.

Although most women can identify their mentors, identifying a sponsor is not as easy. Sponsors are individuals who believe in your value and potential and are prepared to leverage their reputation on your behalf. They have a voice at the decision-making table and will convince others to support you.

Move from mentorship to sponsorship. For all the reasons already highlighted, mentorship is a relevant and a powerful tool; however, to be well-positioned in the professional world, sponsorship is needed to increase the number of women in key leadership roles.

#4 —PARTICIPATION IN TRAINING CAMP

Before the start of the season, athletes engage in training camp. It is a time for them to build relationships with their teammates and learn more about their roles on the team. In the leadership context, training camp comes in the form of leadership development programs. Although women found some value in the content of the leadership development programs, they appreciated the opportunities to network and connect with others outside of their organization.

Leadership development is necessary and imperative for leaders at every level. The goal is to ensure that women are equipped with the essential tools and skills to navigate their professional careers. Participating in leadership development supports women to better understand who they are as leaders and find their niches. A clear understanding of their competencies allows leaders to reinforce their strengths and transform their weaknesses.

Crafting a personalized growth and development learning agenda is pivotal for fostering professional advancement and honing skills:

Develop a growth and development learning agenda.
All women should have an active learning agenda that lists key books, knowledge, and skills that they are committing to grow in their fields. This learning agenda is an individual growth plan that is an alternative to a traditional professional development program. The learning agenda is specifically designed for the leader and targets key areas of learning.

Communicate your learning objectives and proposed participation in training programs to your supervisor, outlining the specific areas you aim to develop; and propose that the organization support your growth initiatives financially. Emphasize the direct correlation between the proposed development and your enhanced efficiency and effectiveness within your current role. Clearly delineate how this investment in your development aligns with improving your performance and contributing positively to your responsibilities within the company.

#5 —PUT POINTS ON THE BOARD
When athletes commit to putting points on the board, they decide to make an impact and get the win! In a professional setting, women put points on the board by choosing to engage in work that is meaningful to them and impactful in their sector.

Black women have historically focused keenly on their abilities to add value to their communities and the people whom they serve. Women are aware of the power and influence they possess as leaders at the executive levels. Women are typically humble and do not take the opportunity to sit in a position of power lightly, believing "to whom much is given, much is required." Although their jobs came with many responsibilities, the women I interviewed were resolute in committing to roles because they viewed the opportunities as ways to lead via their influence on their industries and communities. Additionally, putting points on the board meant leaving a legacy through significant contributions to their fields. In addition to putting points on the board, it is also important for women to build a bench.

#6 —BUILD A BENCH

The power of a strong bench was demonstrated during the 2021 Summer Olympics. Some of the top-performing athletes were unable to compete, requiring the "next man up" to fill the void. The women discussed the importance of building their skills to successfully reach new heights in their careers and the need to build a bench or strong team to support the work and be ready to step up in the event of a transition. This approach is especially true when making space for other Black women. There are so few Black women in senior leadership roles, it is uncommon for them to have peers who are Black women. The women were dedicated to ensuring that they also advocated for other Black women to hold leadership positions. Additionally, the women discussed the need to build a bench in their own families by leaving a legacy.

Establishing a robust professional bench requires strategic steps to cultivate and expand a pool of talented connections, ensuring a bench of skilled women are ready for roles when they are available:

Create a safe space for Black women leaders with aspiring Black women leaders.

Aspiring executive leaders must connect with women who have already ascended to not only learn from them but also build authentic relationships that could lead to mentorships and sponsorships.

Become a sponsor.
As previously mentioned, moving from mentorship to sponsorship is extremely important to increase the number of women in leadership positions. Often decisions are made in advance of posting a role on the company's website. The role is often floated in trusted circles and recommendations

are made. This is our opportunity as women to ensure other women are considered for these roles.

#7 —TO THINE OWN SELF BE TRUE.

Athletes might struggle to compete and lose themselves when they are under pressure to win and perform. The women warned against this, emphasizing the importance of strong senses of self-identity, self-worth, and defined beliefs and philosophies for Black women in senior leadership positions. The key to comprehending these dynamics is to be true to yourself.

Throughout my thesis research, women I interviewed highlighted the need for Black women in top leadership roles to have a strong sense of identity, self-confidence, and established core beliefs. To thy own self be truthful is one of the key dispositions necessary for Black women to further their careers.

I often verbalize to women, "*Know who you are before you enter an organization, or the organization will make you who they want you to be.*" I get to work with a ton of women who are ready for the next step in their career and/or ready to move on from one organization to another. When I ask them what they are looking for in a role and an organization, it is often unclear. It is typically unclear because they have not done their own self-work.

Do the self-work.

Take time to engage in values clarification exercises that force you to learn more about yourself and the lens through which you view the world. Assessments such as Clifton Strengths Finder and Myers-Briggs are helpful in learning more about who you are and the why behind your approach to leadership.

Additionally, making a connection with an organization should be similar to romantic relationships. There should be alignment on fundamental philosophical beliefs and the relationship should be mutually beneficial. The connection should be one in which the individual flourishes as well as the organization.

Rest Up and Jump In

These women were first-round draft picks recruited to their roles because they spent their formative years developing a strong reputation by working hard and making sacrifices to knock it out of the park. Although the women were recruited to their roles, each found herself working hard to prove that she belonged in her respective position, creating an earned, not given mentality. Instead of getting the superstar treatment a first-round draft pick might expect, the participants were marginalized and treated like a walk-on. The women did excellent work; and held to their true selves and did not sacrifice themselves in the process.

Although the interviews revealed that Black women in executive leadership roles have multifaceted experiences, these women prioritized putting points on the board and building a bench. The women committed to engaging in meaningful work that positively impacts their community while ensuring they are mentoring and sponsoring others, particularly other Black women, to secure leadership positions.

Each of us has our own path to forge, littered with barriers and rule changes, but as we make our way, we can clear the path for others. We can commit to removing barriers and lifting others up. We are the new leaders who chose to do better, be better, and not repeat the failures of the past. We are better. We are the leaders now.

INTRODUCING
MARY BETH RITCHEY

Mary Beth Ritchey, BSN, MSPH, PhD, FISPE has spent her career dedicated to better understanding medical product safety and effectiveness within the "real world" where patients are managing new and chronic health conditions in an increasingly complex health care system. She enjoys leading multi-stakeholder international clinical research, strategic planning and coordination of scientific programming, developing actionable policies, and enabling rigorously accurate plain-language information to aid informed decisions about medical products. As Chief Scientific Officer for CERobs Consulting, she leads a team providing innovative strategy and conducting rigorous evidence-generation studies. Additionally, as part-time faculty in the Center for Pharmacoepidemiology and Treatment Science at Rutgers University, she teaches and mentors students who will become future leaders in the field. Dr. Ritchey holds bachelor's degrees in chemistry (Duke University) and nursing (University of North Carolina [UNC] Chapel Hill) as well as Masters and Doctoral degrees in epidemiology from UNC Gillings School of Global Public Health.

She has more than forty peer reviewed publications and book chapters and she co-edited a textbook on pragmatic clinical trials (2021)—this being her first non-technical publication.

Dr. Ritchey has been active in the International Society for Pharmacoepidemiology (ISPE) throughout her career and is the current ISPE President (2023-2024). She is active in her church, currently serving on the Board. Dr. Ritchey is grateful for advice from mentors throughout her career and considers it a privilege and responsibility to do the same for others. She hopes to always be a vocal advocate and cheerleader for those in her sphere to work toward whatever success looks like in their own lives.

Affiliations: Chief Scientific Officer, CERobs Consulting Principal and Owner, Med Tech Epi Associate Research Professor, Center for Pharmacoepidemiology and Treatment Sciences, Institute for Health, Health Care Policy and Aging Research, Rutgers University

LEADERSHIP IS ADVOCACY. ADVOCACY IS LEADERSHIP.

Leadership progression is seemingly simple: first manage yourself, build a team, guide a group, and then steer an organization. I'm not sure what happens after that—conquer the world?

Simon Sinek said we achieve more when we chase the dream instead of the competition. (X, @simonsinek) He also said leadership is not about being in charge—leadership is about looking after those in our charge. Star and high-potential employees want to rise to the top and want individual accolades. Leaders want success for those around them. For me, leadership is helping individuals identify their own definition of success and then creating the space for them to achieve it. Ultimately, the height of leadership is advocacy.

The lessons learned on my journey were difficult. I started out doing things the hard way because I thought that was the only way one achieved success. It was *supposed* to be hard.

In a particularly brutal semester, I took physical chemistry—notoriously the most difficult part of a chemistry major—in one semester instead of two. I got a C-minus, my lowest grade ever. The worst part was I didn't learn any great lessons by doing things the hard way. The only thing I remember about those torrid classes was a story about a man meeting a mountain goat hiking in Scotland, where the man meandered in the fog and then got head-butted off a cliff by the goat—kinda like my semester grade.

Several people tried to steer me away from my hard rocks approach. English teachers encouraged me to pursue my unique writing style, a roommate indicated a linguistics course that I would enjoy, and friends noted my flair for the dramatic. I stuck with the chemistry major. It was only later that I realized it didn't have to be hard—but, reaching personal mastery required me to find my passion and to find my voice.

It took me a long time to find my voice—literally. In elementary school, we presented two mandatory school-wide plays per year and had monthly choir performances.

My tummy twisted when memorizing lines and threatened to empty itself before every performance. I struggled and sputtered through every speech in high school and steered clear of the college courses that required presentations. A professor once interrupted my presentation and asked me not to mumble. Despite all this, the best part of my semester of physical chemistry was the drama class immediately following. Drama provided an outlet for the angst and fear that coursed through me during chemistry class.

After I finished school, I was lucky because my first boss took the time to get to know me and helped me define my career goals. I wanted to lead initiatives and innovate within my field of pharmacoepidemiology. She knew that this goal required technical knowledge, the ability to deliver context, and describe a compelling vision to a wide audience. In other words, I had to master and embrace speaking in front of people.

The opportunities to practice rolled in. I started with leading discussions amongst internal teams and progressed to speeches on scientific topics with external audiences. Eventually, I was articulating programmatic status and defending strategic positions to senior management. And then I led programs, which required presenting major findings, policy, and vision-casting speeches to broad academic and industry audiences. After a couple of years, it was not uncommon for me to have multiple substantive presentations in one week.

It was exhausting. *Every. Single. Time.*

For every presentation, my stomach roiled, my heart pounded, and ridiculously my arms and hands shook before each speech. Then one day, I was presenting a programming update at a conference, and the energy to be both nervous and deliver the material was too much to muster. I succumbed to the most important part and that was delivering the content. When I let go of my angst and fear, I eased into the speech and spoke with my own clear and strong voice.

I found a unique style in my presentations. With all the practice, my voice became part of who I am. I embraced the role and now relish the opportunity to share my vision and expertise publicly. I owe this skill to my first boss who took the time to learn what I wanted to do with my career and then create the space for my growth in an area that *I did not want* to do, but which was needed the most. The best leaders are ones who take the time to understand their team members, their strengths and career aspirations, then encourage mastery through experience and opportunity.

This is what I love about leading others - creating the

space and time to gain proficiency and success. The best leaders in my past helped me find my voice and now I do the same for others.

Leading is daunting and takes patience. It takes time to let a new employee learn a task, check in with them, discuss their progress, and provide empowering feedback. Often, the initial stages of delegating take two or three times as long as doing the task myself. It can take even longer to move through the stages of delegation when the task is complex or has multiple critical objectives or when it occurs infrequently.

Good leaders seek out ways to improve themselves, in order to translate that to their team. For me, my church has proven to be an incubator for development, a safe place to learn and lead. It is an environment that values always improving and striving for betterment. At our weekly gatherings I grow, as I enrich my soul.

Each week a group of volunteers comes together under Guest Services to transform a school or theater venue into a church setting. We greet people at the door, serve coffee, usher people to their seats for services, and then at the end we dismantle the entire setup. I have had the joy of leading our Guest Services team in various capacities over the years. Last year, I reprised the role in a transitory fashion as we were returning to weekly services after COVID and did not have anyone ready to take on that responsibility.

Over six months, we sought out the right person for the role. We needed someone who was comfortable with behind-the-scenes details of scheduling, inventory management, coordination of volunteers, and who was also skillful in engaging and caring for team members. This person had to be proficient in providing necessary information and be able to provide a brief inspirational talk each week.

We did find the right person for the role. She was organized and had a natural talent for connecting with people. But she was nervous to step out and lead.

I understood how she felt, because although now I was authentically excited to give the talk and to lead, my skill was honed over years of practice. Now, I could encourage her to embrace the stretch goal of responsibility as something she needed to learn, just like I had. I deployed the same techniques my old boss and others had used to help me navigate the bigger and scarier responsibilities.

First, we acknowledged the fear and that this was a growth opportunity. She confirmed that the short, inspirational speech was what she was most anxious about doing. We discussed the option to remove it from the role. However, in that discussion we noted it was an important part of the job and she wanted to be able to do it.

We started out by writing a script each week. She read the script and then we debriefed after the gathering. We talked about delivery and cadence, what went well and what needed improvement. We then moved to preparing bullet points. She felt more stilted; this format interrupted her flow, and others noticed her struggling. We then templated out the sections of content to cover each week and created a theme across multiple weeks. The pastor or I drafted bullets within the sections, and she started to provide her own anecdotes.

I shared with her my process for generating the content each week. Then, we switched it up and she began drafting the bullets and anecdotes using the same template. Together we discussed different ways to adjust the template. She grew into the role and now has embraced the short inspirational speech. She has been leading the Guest Services team for eight months and not only is she comfortable, but she is excelling. Leading and learning to lead doesn't just happen in the workplace.

I love that this allowed her to develop a new skill and allowed me to practice my leadership skills. We started with "do exactly this" by reading a script. Then, we moved to a "show how" phase, then to a "report back" phase with the template, bullets, and multi-week themes. And, finally, we moved to a fully delegated task. She has completely taken over the role, including the weekly speech. I am still there if she wants to bounce ideas off of me, but it is her responsibility, and she is inspiring and leading our volunteers.

For me, it was hard to take this activity that I did without much thought and break it down into steps and create a process to hand off to a new person. It was worth it! She has increased skill and capability, which positively impacts the entire organization, and I enjoyed seeing her learn and flourish—I was (and am) her cheerleader! Go team!

The other side of this learning curve is that not everyone wants to be a leader and not everyone wants to constantly strive to improve. This was a difficult lesson for me—why wouldn't everyone always want to better themselves? However, each person has their own definition of success. Leading is helping each person identify her desire for accomplishments and supporting her efforts to achieve them. Finding a way to combine what an individual wants to attain with the triumphs of a team or an organization is where excellent leadership shines.

The first time I was asked to lead a large program, I was assigned a project manager who had no desire to take on additional work. Her goal was to read romance novels for as much of the day as possible. However, when given a concrete task with defined steps, she would accomplish it (with the minimal amount of effort and meeting the minimum bar to sufficiently complete the task). This work ethic was juxtaposed with a desire to be promoted. There was not an option for her to be promoted based on years of service, so accomplishing operational tasks was the primary factor for her advancement.

The two of us sat down and discussed her desire to get a promotion. She shared what she would be able to do because of the promotion and how it fit with her idea of success. I reminded her that I was not her supervisor and did not have the ability to determine whether she would get the promotion, but that I would have the ability to provide feedback based on her work supporting my program.

With the definition of success in mind, we were able to construct a list of duties that she must accomplish and defined the minimum sufficient bar for doing the work. The program was growing, so this was a combination of known tasks and future potential work. We even detailed how she wanted to receive new requests. This was new for me too. I had not thought of how important it was to be specific about how a team member wanted to engage in the work, but now I always incorporate this aspect into conversations when leading people.

Taking the time to define how a team member prefers to engage with her work in an open and frank discussion empowers the person to share her wants and needs and establishes the foundation for her accountability in the future. It also enables a relational connection between colleagues (as opposed to purely transaction-based work). In this case, it meant that I learned about romance novels and how she thought I was working too hard.

We came to an understanding that when I had a new task for her, I would walk by her office. If she was working, I would not interrupt; I would leave the materials for the task on the side of my desk and come back another time. If she was reading, I gave her the task and we reviewed it together—she then completed the task before going back to reading. I came to appreciate that even though she was reading, she was always *ready* to work on any task that came up. By virtue of us taking time to connect in the beginning, she knew that doing the work was leading to her success and I knew that if she was reading, she was willing to take on a new task from me. We tracked her progress, creating a listing of tasks and results to share with her supervisor.

She wanted me to agree to things too. For instance, if

she took on a task, I would not add other tasks to my own workload to replace it. She loved the concept of "taking something off of my plate." She was thrilled to be able to help me and I relished the additional sleep. After a few months, if she saw me walk by her desk early in the day, she would drop by later to see if I had something for her to do. She appreciated that she could work the way *she* wanted; she took ownership, and accepted additional work when needed. If I asked for a task multiple times, she added it to her standing list so then I did not have to ask for it each time.

It was not perfect and was not what I had planned when agreeing to lead the program, but she took on substantially more tasks than she had been doing—sometimes at her own request—and her involvement in the program did give me more bandwidth. In the end, we provided positive results to her supervisor, and she got promoted—achieving her defined measure of success.

I was happy for her—and I loved being the person cheering her on and showing her the path to success. My favorite thing about the entire process was that her attitude changed. She started seeking out work and wanting to be part of the team. For our program, she was always ready to be of support.

Admittedly this is an extreme example. I am not sure

how often leaders are faced with competing with romance novels; more likely today it is Instagram. But, I did take the time to consider a creative and collaborative solution that helped me, her, and the program. This would not always work in every situation. Though, given the context of this situation, this solution worked for everyone involved.

This experience taught me that it is imperative to integrate an individual's success, by her own definition, within the team's success. The agreements and openness at the beginning were critical, as was the routine tracking and monitoring of her progress. With these elements we were both able to see her positive impact on the program.

Finding the spark and fanning the flame empowers everyone to achieve. This type of advocacy for someone to reach her own success occurs both when someone is wanting to stretch into something new and when she is actively avoiding it. This aspect of leadership can be applied to ourselves too, when we want to do something but are afraid to take that next big step.

Writing this chapter has been this type of stretching and learning experience for me. I want to share my story, but the imposter syndrome has been real, overwhelming, and even surprising! The idea of this chapter initially felt so tangible and straight forward, but when facing the blinking cursor on the screen, no words came. I was nearly two months late in getting my draft to the editor. To get through it, I relied on all my writing motivation skills and techniques—early morning writing, notes, outlining, scripting, walking, and talking to get a transcript, writing an hour a day, and blocking out chunks of time to write.

Then, I employed accountability, telling a close friend about the chapter deadline, and the need to finish and submit it. Importantly, I accepted the grace given by the editor and recognized that this seeming impasse did not define me. Next, I waded into a long day of making it happen, with rabbit trails and work emails and last-minute needs from the voices around me and inside my head.

I tell you this for three reasons:

1. Personal mastery is an ongoing effort and is needed for continued progress in leadership;
2. The journey is sometimes not pretty, but you only move forward when you embrace it and muddle through;
3. Evolution in one area does not equate to improvement in all areas.

To achieve one of my own goals I need to write more. I'm thankful for the opportunity to contribute to Brave

Women at Work, and thereby to do this *very hard thing.* I'm embracing it. I'm ready to take that next step. I've found my voice, I'm ready to write!

The best leaders find out what a person's goals are and encourage her to do the things that help her achieve those goals. Leaders provide their team members with opportunities to grow into the persons they want to be. For me, I have learned that I want to create space for individuals and leaders to achieve their own definition of success.

Do the hard things for yourself. Do them for others.

Leadership is advocacy. Advocacy is leadership.

INTRODUCING CHURNI BHATTACHARYA

Churni Bhattacharya is a digital transformation leader with extensive experience in technology transformation, focusing on vision, strategy, roadmap, and implementation to enable best-of-class customer experience and measurable success. She has a proven track record of transforming the legacy landscape into next-generation SaaS (Software as a Service) platforms, transformational change, leadership building, high-performing teams, and delivering outstanding results.

She has worked in financial services for most of her career, focusing on capital markets, commercial banking, mortgage banking, insurance, and wealth management. In doing so, she partnered with C-level executives to define and deliver on technology roadmaps.

Most recently, Churni served as the Chief Application Officer at AssetMark Inc. where she had the responsibility for over 75% of the capital budget of the company, leading the portfolio of strategic initiatives. She has been instrumental in the largest transformational initiatives AssetMark undertook, namely custodial system replacement, implementation of a new tax management system, a new billing system and digital transformation. She also led the productization and agile transformation at AssetMark.

Prior to joining AssetMark, she was the VP, Business Technology Partner for Deposits at First Republic Bank. In that role, she worked as the Divisional Chief Information Officer (CIO), providing end-to-end technology services and experiences for the largest business of the bank.

Prior to the First Republic, she served as the Director of Technology and Project Management Officer (PMO) for the small-business care group at Intuit. She has also worked at Accenture, JMN Consulting, and Ernst & Young. She led a technology strategy initiative for many different Fortune 500 financial services companies. She has delivered numerous large technical implementations.

Interestingly enough, she started her career as a software engineer at Citibank in Tokyo. Churni has an MS in computer science from Pune University, India and a BS in Physics from Jadavpur University, India.

LIFE IS NOT
A STRAIGHT LINE

According to Interactive Mathematics, "*In geometry, a straight line is defined as a line segment that connects two points and extends infinitely in both directions. A straight line is the shortest distance between two points. The straight line is also considered to be the most basic type of line.*"

I love math. Love, love, love it! I loved it when I was in school, and despite having a horrible math teacher the last two years of high school, I am still passionate about math. I am re-learning and re-discovering the joy of math while helping my fifteen-year-old son with his math homework and relishing every moment of it!

A straight line has a geometrical definition: shortest distance between two points and is one dimensional. It is so fundamental to our thinking that it is also an adjective. Here is a definition from Merriam-Webster dictionary:

"Straight-line *adjective*

ˈstrāt-ˈlīn

: being a mechanical linkage or equivalent device designed to produce or copy motion in a straight line

: having the principal parts arranged in a straight line

: marked by a uniform spread and especially in equal segments over a given term

straight-line amortization

straight-line depreciation

: occurring, measured, or made in or along a straight line"

WE PLAN IN STRAIGHT LINES.

In middle school I knew what my career would be. I was one hundred percent certain that I would be a physics professor. No doubt about it—it was going to happen.

At thirteen years old, I was convinced about my career decision for a couple of key reasons. First, I come from a highly educated family of grandparents, aunts, uncles, and cousins with numerous post-doctorate degrees. I have a master's in computer science and am the least educated person in my generation.

Second, and super meaningfully, my coolest uncle

had his PhD in physics and was a professor. There you go. I was set. Get my PhD and teach physics, which two of my younger cousins also planned. Did I mention my uncle was cool?

Point A was me at thirteen; the straight line to Point B was a mid-twenties woman being a professor of physics. I was determined to travel the shortest distance in the shortest amount of time to my goal.

Then life happened.

True to my effort in *straight-lining* my life I studied physics in college. I was getting decent grades and exactly to plan, I was applying to master's programs. I was huddled over the application and reviewing the next set of *straight-line* tasks when a little voice struggled to be heard. *Do you really love physics?*

Ha! Of course! I love physics! I love math! This is my plan. This is the straight line between Point A and Point B.

The little voice wriggled and fought to be heard. I had to acknowledge that maybe I didn't love physics as much as I thought I did, even though my cool uncle did, and my cousins were still studying it. Maybe I was more interested in something else.

My undergraduate introduction to computer science was interesting and engaging. It came naturally and I actually enjoyed the assignments more than anything else. Maybe I should consider computer science for my masters? But what about my Plan and the ever-important Point B?

I completed my Bachelor of Science degree in physics, then I took my first deviation from my Plan into Computer Science.

DEVIATION ONE

Ambition is *"an ardent desire for rank, fame, or power,"* passion is defined as *"intense, driving, or overmastering feeling or conviction,"* and love is defined as *"a great interest and pleasure in something."*

Deviation number one was made on a decision based on love and passion, and not ambition. I realized that I was not as passionate about physics as I thought, but it was my ambition to be a physics professor. Deviating from the Plan required self-assessment and self-reflection about my true interests and passions, not just my desires and ambitions.

But this was only a minor deviation from the Plan; Point C now was a computer science professor instead of a physics professor—easy, no big deal. *Now*, I thought, *my ambition and my passion are aligned.*

After securing my master's and before starting my PhD, I went to work as a software programmer in a consulting company. Oh man! If I thought I loved math—I loved this job even more! I had an absolute blast writing code and building relationships with colleagues. Work was so much more enjoyable than school. The commitments were clearer, and I was getting paid!

After that, deviations to the Plan came tumbling one after another. By my late twenties, I did not have a PhD from an American university, nor a job in teaching. Instead, I was writing software in Tokyo. I was working in the Derivatives Operations Team as a technology coordinator, something I could not even imagine, or knew existed, when I was thirteen years old.

A straight line is one-dimensional—life is not.

CONTINGENCY PLANNING AND RISK MANAGEMENT—ELIMINATING NON-LINEARITY

My ambitious friends and colleagues did not leave things up to chance. They spent time carefully constructing contingencies to mitigate any risks which could upset their Plans.

They created lists of twenty schools to apply to instead of ten, in the event they did not get into the school they wanted. They built fallback Plans casting a wider net for employment and not depending on their first choice. These brilliant folks attempted to force their lives into a straight line, even at the cost of their own passions. Their ambition led the way and was the only voice they heard.

CHOICES WE MAKE—ARE THEY EVEN OUR OWN?

Often our initial life choices and our *straight-line* Plans are not even our own. We make early decisions about life based on what society and our families say is valuable. Often in Western culture this is money, power, and influence. The stack of doctorate family members and my cool uncle had an outsized influence on my Plan. These early life decisions are also commonly based on what we think other people want: a successful neighbor or a media personality—pretending their life is amazing and perfect—or a really cool uncle.

Sadly, many of us feel that love and passion are distractions to our Plans. I posit that these should be the foundation of our Plans. Ambition is a powerful driver, but when do you know you have achieved your Plan if it is solely riding on ambition?

The first deviation from my Plan was to listen to my inner voice. What did I really love and what was I really passionate about? After that first deviation, my passion and inner voice grew and I allowed that to define my path, not ambition. I enjoy my work so much that I lose track of time. Whenever a job stops being fun, I move onto a new one.

Ambition will only get you so far—passion is required for your highest levels of performance and engagement. A+ players are passionate, engaged, and fully committed. They give you everything because their work comes from a place of joy and love. Ambitious people are and can be successful, but it is with their own success in mind, not the success and joy of the work or the organizational vision.

STRAIGHT-LINE POINT B

The number of successful people who burn out is astonishing. Too many times I have seen a colleague or friend experience a midlife crisis, which broke families, killed careers, and disrupted the lives of everyone around the crisis-sufferer. These people were driven, ambitious and successful.

They executed their straight-line plan perfectly and reached Point B. And then they could not figure out Point C, thus could not answer the question *Now what?*

They had no purpose, no passion, and thought, "*Is this it? Is this what life is supposed to be?*"

THE LEADERSHIP CONVERSATION
ABOUT PASSION

The art of feedback is similar to raising a dog. When you only focus on corrections and harsh criticisms, you raise an anxious, fearful, and an eventually aggressive dog. When you provide positive reinforcement with lots of love and T-R-E-A-T-S, then you have a confident, happy, and healthy dog.

Humans are not that different.

Leaders have a responsibility to ignite and sustain passion for their team members. As a leader, I am acutely aware of two things: first, I am in a position of power; and second, people are always watching me.

Being in a position of power, I have the ability and responsibility to raise happy and healthy team members. I am responsible for my team's wellbeing and ensuring they perform to their fullest potential. I provide a steady diet of feedback, positive and opportunistic, based on our mutual understanding that I am doing it to help them improve. I highlight areas of improvement but more importantly, I tell people what they are doing well. Positive reinforcement is key to ensuring a high performing team.

I ask these two questions always when performing reviews and developing people: "Where does your passion lie?" and "Where do you see yourself in the future (5, 10, or

15 years)? I am always floored by how many people struggle to answer these seemingly simple questions. These questions are crucial to ignite passion in team members and to attempt to align their current role and assignments with their passion. Importantly, these questions allow me to assess any potential for burn-out and to help my team members answer their *now what* question.

These cannot just be your words; this must be your demonstrated reality. If I ask my team members this without my passion fueling my work-life, then I am a fraud. If I am not seen as genuinely having fun, nobody will listen to the words coming out of my mouth, however wise they may sound. Leaders must practice what they preach; and strong, happy, passionate leaders build high performing teams who have fun while working hard.

AUTHENTIC SUCCESS IS NOT A STRAIGHT LINE.

My husband and I love to go for long drives. The windier the road, the more fun it is. The drives are never a straight line. They take us up hills, into valleys, switchbacks, twists, and turns. We don't always drive to some renowned peak that provides a beautiful view, but even when we do, we are enjoying the entire journey, not just the mountain top. The lush green valleys are as amazing as the expansive view afforded at the top.

In fact, sometimes the valleys are more interesting than the peaks. For a peak to be truly a peak, there is only one way to go, down! And, while you are going down, you start thinking about the next peak to conquer.

Valleys are instructive because there is only one way to go—up! Valleys are the preparation time for the next mountain top. Valleys are our teaching grounds. We catch our breaths in the valleys and get stronger and wiser.

Peaks change over time. When you are coming down, it feels one way. But the farther you walk away from the peak, the sky looks different and there is different light; the peaks look different too.

Fifteen years ago, I used to describe the high points of my career in a completely different way than I do now. Same peaks but they are so different than they were when I was on them and in the years following them.

In 1999 I achieved an incredible implementation of a new software platform. The implementation was a grand achievement, on time, on budget, and delivered on all stated goals. Now I feel that the entire business case was flawed and there were so many things I would do differently. At the time, and for the years following, it felt like an awesome accomplishment; but now not so much.

The definition of success changes over time based on the subsequent peaks and valleys you move through.

THE LEADERSHIP CONVERSATION
ABOUT FAILURES

I cherish my failures because not only did they teach me more than my successes, they changed me and made me a better me. Each time they also taught me about what is most important to me and allowed me to reassess my love and passion, an important element that I learned to follow with the first deviation from my Plan.

As I tell my teams, remember to celebrate successes, but reserve high-value treats for failures. Too many times, in the name of root-cause analysis and retrospectives, leaders assign blame and throw people under the bus when they encounter failures. This is a terrible practice and only leads to infighting, unhealthy competition, skirting the truth and hiding failures.

Instead of *Why did we fail?* The question should be *What did we learn from this?* It is not *Who messed up?* but *Who helped others?* Life is not a straight line, and it is never traveled alone.

Great leaders build and empower their teams and team members. They know the value of resting and recharging and supporting individuals and colleagues through their own valleys. Bad leaders end up alone.

POINT B—OR POINT QQQ, DEPENDING ON HOW YOU COUNT THE DEVIATIONS

Looking back at my journey, I am grateful that I chose to listen to my inner voice gently questioning if I love physics? That first deviation allowed me to identify my loves and passions and build a joyful and triumphant career in leadership on those foundations. I did not slog unhappily through my career and solely depend on ambition. Ambition leads to burning out and leaves the individual questioning *What now?* and *Is this it?*

Leading from the heart takes courage and grace, and a willingness to fail. These valleys in life lead to the next successful mountain top, but all the while enjoying the journey and applying the learnings to the next climb.

If you haven't done so, I encourage you to reflect on your love and passions and let them lead you. The sooner you do, the happier, more fulfilled, and more successful your life and career will be. Work from a place of passion and joy, not just ambition.

INTRODUCING SHELIA HIGGS BURKHALTER

Shelia Higgs Burkhalter, affectionately known as "Shiggs," is a bestselling author, an accomplished speaker, facilitator, and a certified Executive & Leadership Transitions Coach with 30 years of experience in the higher education sector. Shelia is committed to creating inclusive, collaborative, and excellence-driven campus communities that inspire and position students to engage, transform, and thrive.

Recognized as a 2023 NASPA Pillar of the Profession by the NASPA Foundation (National Association of Student Personnel Administrators), Shelia has played a pivotal role in student affairs and higher education. Her active engagement with NASPA, particularly in areas focusing on career pipelines, advancement, women, first-generation populations, and diverse communities, underscores her dedication to impactful contributions.

Shelia specializes in guiding aspiring executives and leaders through successful transitions, placing a strong emphasis on people, values, and leading with heart. As the founder and owner of ShiggsB Coaching, LLC, she integrates her extensive knowledge of leadership, communication, and energy to create a transformative experience for her clients.

In addition to her coaching endeavors, Shelia co-authored the book chapter "Taking the Job Search to the Next Level" in *Careers in Student Affairs: A Holistic Guide to Professional Development in Higher Education* in 2017. Furthermore, in July 2022, she contributed chapter one, titled "First, Only, Different" to the Amazon best-selling book *Brave Women at Work: Stories of Resilience.* In that chapter, she emphasized the foundational role of values in making authentic and joyful life choices.

Shelia holds a Managerial MBA from the University of Arkansas, Fayetteville; an MSEd in Student Affairs Administration from Indiana University, Bloomington; and a BS in Mass Communication-Political Science from Southeast Missouri State University. Her academic achievements complement her wealth of practical experience, contributing to her holistic approach to coaching and leadership development.

MEET THE MOMENT

"Courage is the most important of all the virtues, because without courage you can't practice any other virtue consistently."
— Maya Angelou

I am compelled to act, to solve a problem, to name injustice, to fix brokenness, to make things better, to be a bridge, to advocate, to give voice to those without one, to speak truth to power, and to deliver. Sometimes that compulsion is a tug, at other times it is a push, sometimes it is a feeling within my gut, and at other times it is a whisper in my spirit. At all times, it is an undeniable need to *meet the moment.*

For me, meeting the moment is typically not about one big moment. It is a series of small moments that matter day to day, year after year. Occasionally those small moments culminate in a bigger moment. This story is a series of small moments that led to a big public, meet the moment event.

People streamed into the law school, a building made entirely of glass, exchanging greetings with friends and colleagues. Some veered right, racing to the bowels of the building using the lightning-fast elevators. Others walked straight ahead and down the stairs past the reflecting pool meant to calm spirits and invoke serenity. The Town Hall on budget was being held and everyone was interested in hearing the final fund distribution. For weeks there had been discussions, murmurs, and whispers about the closed-door conversations happening across campus. Today was the day everyone would learn the outcome of those closed-door sessions.

Three hundred people—faculty, staff, and students—entered the Moot Courtroom, giving proof of the level of interest in what was to be revealed in the meeting. There was anticipation etched on people's faces as they fidgeted and tried to settle into their seats. Senior leadership had been poring over profit and loss sheets and confidentially discussing budget cuts for months. With precipitous drops in enrollment and state-mandated, but unfunded increases to benefits and the state pension pool, we were facing our eighth round of budget reductions in eight years. The University had cut all the fat and most of the muscle of university budgets and were now down to the bone. We were in marrow territory, and the people entering that room wanted to know from where that marrow would be taken.

In those eight years of budget reductions all employees endured an institution-wide furlough, the elimination of vacant positions, and hiring freezes. Positions were only filled if they were directly tied to compliance, revenue generation, or full-time instruction. Several occupied "nonessential" positions were eliminated leading to layoffs; adjunct faculty lines were cut; and early retirements were offered and accepted. Senior leaders were subjected to pay reductions without their agreement and without the benefit of days off because we were "essential" to the institution's functions. This lack of time away added another black mark into the low morale column. Some programs and services were cut, and others were defunded or modified. The institution was on life support and people were concerned about what and who would be left standing.

Nestled in the heart of the city, the University of Baltimore serves as a second chance campus for many. It offers an opportunity for education, a chance for a better and different life, ultimately creating pathways to an elevated existence. The campus primarily catered to transfer students and adults. A significant number of our students juggled full-time jobs during the day, dedicating their evenings, nights, and weekends to attending classes. Approximately fifty percent of our students were pioneers in their families. First-generation college students forging into new territory to create new legacies. Some students hailed from challenging areas within the city where poverty and need were pervasive.

The college experience with its inherent pressures and adjustments, often spurred common mental health challenges such as anxiety, stress, and depression. For those navigating the intersections of various identities and roles, the prevalence of mental health challenges and the need for support was even more pronounced. The significance of the Division of Student Affairs and its multi-faceted support mechanisms cannot be overstated. While crucial for all universities, it played an especially vital role for our diverse student body.

As budgetary constraints were addressed, the Division of Student Affairs underwent a reduction from its original forty-two-person team to a more streamlined group of twenty-two. Faced with these circumstances, I urged my Student Affairs Leadership Team (SALT) to tap into their creativity and innovation to consider how we'd safeguard essential elements of the student-facing experience amid changes. We needed to preserve programs, services, and initiatives with a direct impact on the daily lives of students. We still had a duty and responsibility to embody the mission statement, collectively crafted and committed to "helping students persist and thrive in their journey toward graduation and transformation while preparing them for their roles as future professionals and community leaders."

Guiding the Student Affairs Leadership Team (SALT), I emphasized the importance of shielding our students from the harsh realities of the budget crisis. This involved moderating and carefully choosing our words, especially in the presence of student workers who served as a direct extension of our professional team and reflected our collective morale.

Recognizing that student workers took cues from our behavior, it was crucial to avoid signaling any uncertainty about the institution's future. If we hinted at potential challenges, our students might adopt that narrative and succumb to panic. Despite the internal concerns and worries of our team, it was imperative to project a sense of calm and steadiness for our students. Leading through this challenge with composure became paramount.

We had difficult choices to make and fewer people

with whom to make them. Our collective morale was at a low point. Yet, somehow, we persevered, rallying together and taking ownership of our choices as a team, rather than leaving them to external decision-makers. As my team modeled and submitted detailed budget cuts ranging from five to twenty-five percent, our focus remained steadfast on prioritizing students.

The initial changes were already having a negative impact, and further alterations would exacerbate the situation. Our responsibility was to ensure transparency regarding the devastation that could ensue should we activate some of these choices. Our team took the initiative to draft and submit reduction impact statements, even though there was uncertainty about whether anyone would read them. I submitted them anyway. These statements served a purpose for the team, acting as a guidepost to maintain our focus on students and the future. It compelled us to thoroughly define and prepare for the worsening situation.

Over time, we streamlined the operations of two units, reduced programming budgets, and increased student fees, all while trimming down student programming. This strategic approach allowed us to preserve the essential framework required to address salient student needs, including compliance, safety, security, well-being, risk mitigation, and career preparation. We responded to the various demands and continued serving our students to the best of our abilities. However, the toll was evident. We were wounded, mere shadows of our former selves. And it was about to get worse.

Ultimately, we had to implement the twenty-five percent reduction. This meant that we cut *everything* we had meticulously modeled, and it was painful. It still wasn't enough. More was needed. The upcoming budget Town Hall would unveil even more decisive cuts. People couldn't fathom what those measures might be or where they would originate.

I'd been on an emotional roller coaster for weeks, listening to academic deans and vice presidents discuss various ideas for restructuring both their own and other colleagues' divisions. During a particularly disheartening moment, an academic dean audaciously suggested that the entire Division of Student Affairs was unnecessary and should be eliminated, minimizing the impact on Academic Affairs and other "essential" divisions. I was typically not easily offended in a professional setting, but I found myself outraged. It was evident to me that he had a myopic perspective of the university with little awareness of the crucial role that Student Affairs played on a college campus.

I met this moment and could not remain silent in the face of his ignorance and blatant disregard for our work. I don't remember exactly what I said, but it went something like this.

"If Academic Affairs is the brain of the institution, then Student Affairs is the heart. We are a stealthily moving force that is the lifeblood of this campus. What we do in silence away from the eyes and awareness of the average person, keeps this University humming along. It keeps student issues off your doorsteps and out of your classrooms. If you cut this division, the impact will be swift and sustained. The institution will be overrun with student issues including behavioral concerns, mental health crises, health and wellness concerns, and food and housing insecurity. Think about the Title IX issues, conflict, stress, accessibility concerns, gaps in academic and social support, recruitment and retention concerns, and difficulty onboarding new students. Not to mention compliance concerns at the state and federal level, and an inability to support students as they launch into their careers. Are the faculty, staff, and administrators of this University ready to take that on?"

They were not.

In that moment, he retreated, but the long slog of negotiations and decisions continued.

While cutting the entire Division of Student Affairs off the table, discussions about the removal of individual units were not. One unit was repeatedly being discussed for possible elimination.

I convened and led a work group to assess alternative solutions with the hope that the results would remove the worst option from consideration. I co-chaired the group with a faculty member and engaged key colleagues—administrators, faculty, and staff—from across the university who had a vested interest in the outcome. We compiled national and institution-level data and discussed the impact of the various options.

Ultimately, the working group presented three alternatives to the Provost and offered a robust, clearly preferred recommendation grounded in our comprehensive research and findings.

Our preferred recommendation was not accepted.

As we gathered data for the proposal, our inquiries began to raise red flags within the team. While I couldn't disclose the specifics of our ongoing work, I remained an advocate, supporter, and fierce protector of my team. The unit's director approached me with questions, and I responded with as much transparency as possible, adhering to the explicit prohibition on sharing budget details or high-level discussions with team members.

"Is our unit being cut?" my director inquired.

"No decision has been made to cut this unit," I replied honestly. "We are reviewing and discussing data on a variety of units across the University."

"Should I be worried about my job?"

"Honestly, I am worried about everyone's jobs, including mine, given the number of cuts that must be made."

"I have been approached with another opportunity by another university," she confided. "A trusted colleague has asked me to apply. What do you think? Should I do it?"

"I think that it is always important to keep your full range of options open," I found myself saying. I did not want her to leave, but what was good for her was more important than my own concerns or those of the university. "If the opportunity feels good to you and you think you'd enjoy working for this person and that institution, there is no harm in applying."

"Would you give me a good reference?"

"Absolutely, you do amazing work and I'd be honored to tell others about how fantastic I think you are," I answered without hesitation.

"Thank you for talking with me about this."

"You are welcome. My pleasure."

"One last question, can I send someone else to talk with you?"

"Of course," I confirmed.

At every decision point, I tried to keep in mind that our team and organization consisted of individuals with emotions, values, responsi-bilities, and commitments that extend beyond their contributions to the workplace. I knew that, in university settings in particular, many employees view their roles as a calling, often foregoing more lucrative opportunities to serve the mission of aiding students in their success.

Recognizing that Student Affairs staff often perceive their work as a meaningful vocation in service to the mission, it is important for me to prioritize their well-being: not only because it fosters a positive work environment and strengthens organizational commitment, but because it is an important value for me. Similarly, being transparent and considerate in my leadership practices builds trust and encourages a sense of shared purpose, ultimately contributing to the overall success of my staff and the institution. The team found their release in offices, behind closed doors by commiserating with trusted colleagues. We sought solace from spouses, mentors, and friends which fortified us to continue the fight.

Though this specific circumstance constrained my ability to be as transparent and direct as I desired, I couldn't ignore the potential consequences of our proposal. I chose to navigate the situation with a leadership approach grounded in care, integrity, and centering my employees' well-being knowing that it could lead to their untimely departures.

The Town Hall meeting began in the Moot Courtroom and the audience quieted. People sat attentively listening as the President and Provost shared the various ways that the institutional budget would be adjusted—again. Some of what was shared was not new territory. There would be more reductions to adjunct faculty positions, elimination of staff lines, the sale of a parcel of land, reductions in programming, travel, marketing, supply, and food budgets, etc. Those reductions were still not enough to balance the budget, so the presentation continued.

The temperature rose in the room and the collective chatter increased as the President suggested that we would explore the possibility of consolidating two colleges. This was not a new idea but had not yet been stated publicly. This was another sign that this was not a typical reduction process. A collective gasp rolled through the auditorium even as the President and Provost were trying to reassure the audience that they were only exploring this idea and it was not a foregone conclusion.

Then, they got to the Division of Student Affairs. I sat, eyes forward, feet grounded, back straight, gritting my teeth in anticipation of the announcement. "The Counseling Center will be closed," the Provost announced.

The audience erupted and clamored for clarity. It seemed everyone was talking at once attempting to confirm what they just heard. Then several hands shot into the air.

The Provost had to field a barrage of questions.

- "Who will assist with events and issues in real time? Where do I take students during a crisis?
- "Where do I take a student who has threatened suicide or talked about other self-harm?"
- "How in an era where students nationwide are seeking mental health services on campus with greater frequency, and on-campus services are the recommended practice, have we dared to make this choice?"
- "How does the school plan to address and prevent increased liability for the university that doesn't have on-campus mental health support?"
- "Who will support our vulnerable students, many of whom are from underserved communities, navigate the stress of college?"
- "Who will provide the knowledge that licensed mental health therapists offer the campus Care and Threat Assessment Team?"

Once the decision was made to close the Counseling Center and long before announcing it at the Town Hall, the dean of students and I engaged a company that could provide virtual mental health support program for the campus. By the time the multitude of inbound reference checks arrived for our two Counselors who were actively job searching, virtual support was established and ready to be deployed.

Before the Town Hall, I created talking points for the leadership team's reference in preparation for these very questions. The talking points detailed the work group, the explored options, the intention to continue to offer mental health support, information about the new virtual mental health resource, and a request to support the Counseling Center professional staff through the transition. Both counselors had secured other positions and tendered their resignations after sensing the direction the institution was headed.

Despite having the talking points in hand, the President and Provost struggled to address the concerns of the audience. Initially, I kept my seat and merely observed the verbal fallout. As the volume increased and the crowd grew more agitated, I slipped a copy of the talking points to the Provost, then whispered a response in the President's ear. He asked me to state the answer directly, then I returned to my seat. The volley of questions continued, and the President and Provost continued to stumble.

When it was suggested by the Provost that the precipitating factor for the Counseling Center closing was the departure of the two Psychiatrists, I had enough. I would not sit and allow anyone to use the Counselors as a scapegoat for this decision.

It was important that people's concerns be met with an ethic of care, empathy, clarity, and information. That was not happening.

I strode to the podium and asked the President if he would like me to field any remaining questions. He quickly agreed and yielded the podium to me.

I met the moment with a quick prayer, *Please God word my mouth*, a deep breath, and stepped to the podium. I put on my communication hat and set the record straight. The departure of the Counselors was not the reason for the closing of the Center then took questions from the audience.

As I answered the questions, I tried to strike a balance between accepting senior leadership's choice, acknowledging the concerns of the stakeholders, supporting my staff, centering students, and providing information about the new resource that would be adopted for the campus and our students.

I held space for the audience as they unleashed their anger, fear, concerns, disappointment, anxieties, stress, and any other feelings that needed a home. I took proverbial shots to my body and mind that were not mine to take because that is what was needed in the moment, and that is what leaders do—meet the moment.

People stopped me as I departed to thank me for my leadership and candor. I left exhausted and carried the weight of the people in that room and a campus that deserved better. A few counseling psychology faculty assured me that they had Student Affairs' back and would be sending a strongly worded email to the President about this decision. Others dropped by the office to tell me that I was "brilliant" in the Town Hall and to thank me for my advocacy and support. Both the Provost and the President dropped by to thank me for handling the questions so eloquently and with grace thereby helping to instill a sense of calm.

In the days and weeks to come, the campus continued to express their concern and angst over the choice to close the Counseling Center. The Faculty of the Applied Psychology-Counseling Psychology Program wrote a beautifully worded appeal to the President with statistics imbedded. A variety of people scheduled appointments and sent communications, but the decision was not rescinded. A couple of months after the Town Hall, the Counseling Center closed. A few months after that, I too announced my departure.

In her article, "How to Meet the Moment and Rise to the Occasion," Dr. Alice Boyes states, "the term 'meeting the moment' is often used to refer to courage in unexpected circumstances" (Psychology Today, July 13, 2022). This definition rings true. But "meeting the moment" is so much more expansive for me.

It means advocating for the stakeholders who were not present; being courageous in the face of opposition; speaking truth to power; using my seat at the table in service to others; offering solutions and alternatives to managing a challenging situation; doing what is right even when a less gracious response felt warranted; shouldering the burdens of others; instilling a sense of calm during crisis; and delivering results under trying conditions.

There is often no rule book for meeting the moment as "moments" can crop up at any time. But there are competencies that can be developed along the way. Here are a few suggestions.

Own your seat at the table. Imposter syndrome is real and will visit you often when you experience adversity, but you have the seat because you have what it takes to occupy it. Speak up and speak out. If not you, then who?

Be an expert in your work. During a crisis there may be very little time to do deep research. Stay abreast of your work and commit to knowing it at an expert level. The muscle memory of what is needed in the moment will download for you when you need it, if you have uploaded it.

Leverage your strengths. Often when we find ourselves in a challenging situation, thoughts about what we are not or what we don't have can rob us of our confidence. Instead take stock of your assets and leverage your strengths to mitigate areas of challenge. This will serve you well when you need to meet the moment.

Lead with authenticity. Get clear about who you are and how you want to walk your talk and embody your values as a leader. Values are a brilliant, ever-present compass. We just need to access them.

Find ways to center yourself. When in the midst of a moment, you can easily feel frazzled and unfocused. Take a minute to center yourself. That could be a quick prayer, a favorite song, a series of deep breaths, a quick walk, etc. Find what works for you and have it ready.

Practice meeting the moment. Every day presents us with opportunities to meet the moment. In some situations, the stakes are low. If I challenge this person's perspective on this issue, they may not like it and they'll be unhappy for a period. At other times the stakes may be high. If I publicly challenge this idea, then I could lose my job. Start out small and build up to bigger moments as you become more confident.

I challenge you to be ready and meet the moment when called to do so. Great leadership requires unparalleled commitment and preparation, and courage to meet the moment. Meet your moment and be your full and powerful self.

INTRODUCING
ECHELL EADY

Dr. Echell Eady has served for more than 25 years at the intersection of workforce development, social services, and postsecondary education. She is the owner and lead consultant at Eady Consulting Group. A nationally certified Career and Education Advisor, Dr. Eady develops strategies for reducing barriers, advancing economic empowerment, and promoting family education, including adult student attainment of postsecondary certificates and degrees.

As a first-generation college graduate, Dr. Eady feels especially well-equipped to serve at-risk, marginalized, and underrepresented populations. She has been recognized for Outstanding Professional Service to the Career Guidance Center (Region 8), Illinois State Board of Education-Adult Vocational and Technical Education. In addition, she has served on her state's

Workforce Development Board under two governors and has volunteered for agencies including the Tennessee Rehabilitation Center, Big Brothers Big Sisters, Junior Achievement, and Books from Birth.

Dr. Eady's authenticity and respect for all has helped her succeed in a multitude of settings. Her community building skills led to the tripling of service delivery for her county's primary youth mentoring program. Dr. Eady is an alumna of several leadership programs including Young Leaders Nashville, Leadership Rutherford, and Complete Tennessee Leadership Institute.

Dr. Eady curates an extensive Barbie collection and enjoys traveling, reading, and film noir. She and her husband Sean are the proud parents of three sons (Tony, Ryan, and Ross), and she's a doting GiGi to her granddaughter, Dani Ariyah Eady.

LET THE INTROVERTED LEADER FILL YOUR CUP

"To become truly great, one has to stand with people, not above them."
—Montesquieu

I remember with fondness the first time I felt like an effective leader. It was in a well-established national non-profit organization where I led four distinct programs. I knew I was honoring my gifts because each day at work felt like play. Being in community with my teams or the greater organization felt safe and affirming. Our collective playtime led to exceeded benchmarks, greater impact, and increased success for our students and clients. Looking back on that experience, I can hardly suppress my amusement at all the advantages I took for granted during the three and a half years spent with that employer.

It would take another, very different experience—an ordeal, actually—to reveal to me that while I can be a highly engaging, effective, and inspirational leader, I struggle when the appropriate support is not in place for myself and for my teams. This contrasting experience was originally presented as a remarkable opportunity. Although I was asked by the leadership to apply to the position, I participated with other candidates in a rigorous selection process. I was elated when I was selected for the job. It was heartbreaking to leave an amazing team and inspirational supervisors behind, but I was convinced that eliminating my two-hour commute and returning to postsecondary education full time was the right move for me and my career at the time. Little did I know that I was embarking upon a horrible leadership experience.

A cameo appearance by the *Twilight Zone*'s host Rod Serling would have befitted the impending saga. For more than three years, I was subjected to bullying and sabotage, followed by gaslighting the few times I complained. I often contemplated stepping away. However, allegiance to my faculty, and an unhealthy dose of pride, kept me in place. It would be an understatement to say that I was treated poorly throughout this experience. Still, there were a few positive outcomes. For example, I led and supported some of the most talented, dedicated faculty anywhere. Externally, I made strides in promoting the school's academic programs. Internally, I became a trusted confidant to others experiencing similar workplace trauma.

As fate would have it, my last day with this employer came as a complete surprise to me. Early one Friday morning, the college President called me into his office where two representatives from Human Resources were waiting. From behind his desk, the President read a list of what he perceived as my shortcomings. I was not allowed a copy of this list. I was given the option of submitting my resignation by end-of-day or being terminated on the spot. I resigned. Their final attempt at humiliation came when they escorted me from the building.

Of course, the entire experience reeked of impropriety. Several close colleagues, former coworkers, and friends strongly encouraged me to seek legal counsel. But I knew that my time and energy would be best spent navigating my next opportunity and focusing on re-centering my gifts and talents. In the midst of all the shadiness and treachery, my time there added clarity to my leadership values. I was humbled but remained committed to the idea of being a service leader.

In my assessment, leadership is about ensuring people feel seen, heard, understood, and appreciated. I often remind the professionals I mentor that, just because someone doesn't understand you, doesn't mean you're not brilliant. Quite the contrary. Sometimes we must be satisfied with comprehending concepts long before others are ready to receive the knowledge. For example, the fact that one doesn't understand Trigonometry in no way invalidates the subject of Trigonometry itself. Similarly, we must resist allowing others' lack of comprehension to invalidate our individual contributions. Be like Trigonometry.

When given the choice between authority and influence, I've always preferred utilizing influence. I enjoy influential interactions, and I'm good at them. There is a natural flow for me when I'm able to persuade rather than demand. Others also seem to enjoy persuasive interactions as well. So many leaders I have observed over the years seem to be on a mission as opposed to answering a call. Oftentimes, the mission has more to do with personal ambition than with the collective good.

I'm convinced that many of the opportunities I've had to lead were born out of my clear lack of desire to take the reins. In fact, as far back as graduate school, I can recall receiving the occasional message that perhaps I shouldn't aspire to leadership at all. To be fair, I'm admittedly a conflict-avoidant introvert (McGregor Theory Y—generally believing the best about employees) who enjoys pleasant, serene interactions, especially at work. Frankly, I don't believe any of the above-mentioned traits render me an insufficient leader. On the contrary, I believe it is exactly these qualities that enhance my leadership contributions. However, certain conditions must exist for my brand of leadership to flourish and yield the highest level of effectiveness.

Before we delve into the eight basic tenets by which I lead, let's first examine how a working-class, poverty-afflicted skinny little Black girl from the Southside of Chicago ever gained access into leadership spaces in the first place. Because I now understand that many of my leadership gifts are borne of my own early experiences, it is imperative that these experiences be examined.

There are several basic leadership traits that I learned by simply surviving my childhood on Chicago's Southside. My resilience, resourcefulness, reservedness, and recognition that *no* means *not yet*, are all qualities developed from early life experiences watching my mother repeatedly "make a dollar out of fifteen cents" as the colloquial saying goes.

I credit my mother with creating the illusion of possibility throughout my childhood. Although my dad has always been in my life, my parents' separation when I was eight years old, and subsequent divorce when I was sixteen, played an enormous role in shaping my formative years. The absence of my dad, particularly his monetary resources, immediately reduced our family's financial status from working-class to poor.

My childhood memories are sprinkled with recollections of food stamps, utility cut-offs, and the ubiquitous government cheese. Throughout all these setbacks, my mother and paternal grandmother worked together to fill my time with opportunities such as dance classes, piano and violin lessons, live theater, and Catholic schools. These experiences were wildly out of place for my socio-economic situation. In fact, one of the defining moments of my childhood was when, prompted by a classmate's query earlier that day, I asked my mother if we were rich. She responded with a chuckle and resounding no.

My mom, having left high school prior to completion, was determined to see her children have a better life than she'd experienced. Although I'm certain the term was not yet known to us, self-efficacy has always played a huge and important role in my life, long before I was familiar with the concept. Self-efficacy describes an individual's belief in their ability to execute specific behaviors that will lead to desired performance outcomes. For example, I am convinced that my status as a first-generation college graduate is in large part due to the self-efficacy that was instilled in me throughout my childhood.

When I finally decided to pursue formal leadership training through a doctoral program in Education with a concentration in Leadership and Professional Practice, I had been in the workforce for several years and was already benefiting from the outstanding tutelage of many wonderful leaders. My doctoral experience was akin to flipped classroom learning whereby students become familiar with lessons first at home; teacher-led instruction in the classroom follows. Similarly, I was bringing lived experiences into a program that would eventually name and organize the lessons to which I'd been exposed throughout my early career.

I have no doubt that many of the civic and community-based leadership opportunities for which I've been recruited have come precisely because I exhibited no inclination to take over. The most notable of these opportunities was my brief stint as PTO President for the top high school in our state at that time. No pressure, right? You will recall that introverts thrive outside of the spotlight. Honestly, a quiet place, a preferred beverage, and a good book form the basis of a perfect day in my estimation; a tropical locale and temperate weather are always welcome additions.

I would be remiss not to mention the importance of any leader's own personal support system, beginning with their direct supervision. My leadership has flourished most often when my upline leaders have been confident, competent, and visionary.

We've often heard that it's impossible to pour from an empty cup. When considering how your staff will respond to customer, client, or student needs; remember to ensure your staff members have full cups from which to pour. By overworking and under-acknowledging your own employees, you are all but guaranteeing they will not be equipped to offer the services best representative of your organization. Following are eight important rules I use as the North Star of my leadership journey. I hope the ideas will be useful for you, the reader, as well.

BE AUTHENTIC

An effective method for building and sustaining trust in the workplace is by always presenting authentically. Naturally, there is a certain decorum by which leadership is expected to abide within their organization. Those expectations aside, showing one's authentic self at work is recommended as team building, culture enhancing behavior. People appreciate knowing what to expect with each interaction. Authenticity evokes trustworthiness.

An added bonus to being authentic is that one never has to recall which persona to present to which team member. Furthermore, authenticity begets authenticity. Team members are empowered to be themselves in the presence of leadership. For these and other reasons, authenticity is a very liberating practice.

PRIORITIZE CULTURE

The axiom is true that workplace culture is how employees feel on Sunday night when they think of Monday morning. To be sure, workplace culture may occasionally, albeit temporarily, be enhanced with donuts, coffee, and trinkets. However, low investment tends to yield low return. Creativity is imperative when crafting an attractive and sustainable company culture. Many organizations now offer release time for employees to volunteer; some operations plan group opportunities to lunch or travel together. Remember, sometimes it's the little pleasantries that, when repeated often, have a sustaining effect on organizational culture.

Conversely, in the interest of optics, employees are encouraged to pretend that everything is fine, even in the face of extreme duress. Less confident leaders can be notorious perpetuators of toxic positivity in the workplace. Unfortunately, being mandated to feign cheerful emotions in the face of oppression can feel subversive, dismissive, and discouraging to staff.

Other questions to consider when focusing on creating a positive work culture include the following: Are employees often bombarded with "emergency" correspondence upon arriving to the office each day? Are staff meetings heavier on admonishments than compliments and appreciation? Does leadership remember to praise in public and correct in private? These are a few "culture busters" that are relatively simple and low-to-no cost to avoid.

SEE EVERYONE

Over the years as I've worked under and alongside a variety of leadership styles, I've discovered that there are some leaders who believe they should see everything. Well, I believe it is far more critical to see *everyone*. When people feel seen (and of course heard) a particular brand of relational loyalty is developed. One of the most important compliments I have ever received came in the form of an Oscar nod from my CEO. Yes, as part of the amazing work culture she constantly curated, my CEO celebrated Hollywood's Oscar season with movie-themed awards for her leadership team. To this day, I proudly display my statue and winning envelope on my fireplace mantle. I was awarded the "Oscar" for Hidden Figures with the following statement: This award goes to the team member that shows perseverance despite the odds. This star has taken on particularly expansive, exhausting projects and makes them work. Wow. Talk about feeling seen—and appreciated.

Because leadership is a calling for me, I can see the vision and I see each team member clearly and individually. I take immense pride in being able to recognize team members for who they are and for what they contribute. It is important to draw out and nurture gifts and talents so that the talents can then be channeled toward the appropriate goals and outcomes. It does little to no good to attempt to press and contort everyone into the same operational mold simply to fit a leader's preferred style. Much better outcomes are achieved by allowing each team member to walk in their greatness while directing that greatness toward the most appropriate contribution.

Band directors and orchestra conductors have the right idea. Listen to a violin hum, a piccolo peep, a timpani thunder. The best musical directors combine the greatest sounds from each individual instrument into a delightful tapestry of sound. Imagine if each of these instruments was expected to make the exact same sound because the band or orchestra director preferred, or was familiar with, only one way of creating music.

EXTEND GRACE

Leadership implies followership; in the workplace, these followers are human beings. As such, staff on any given day will no doubt present us with very human problems. How we as leaders respond to our employees makes all the difference in their confidence and trust in us, as well as in the overall culture of an organization. When we as leaders react harshly in the face of our employees' personal hardships, we inadvertently send the message that we do not see them as human beings and that we do not care about them outside of any direct benefit they have to our workplace agenda. Leading with kindness is not the same as leading with weakness.

In the workplace, strivers and self-starters are easy for most leaders to appreciate. However, contributions will not always present in the form of ambition. When coaching an employee who exhibits no obvious aspirations, I shift my focus to their particular *WHY* regarding the team specifically and the organization as a whole. Often, employees who don't appear especially energetic about their responsibilities can experience renewed enthusiasm when encouraged to reflect on their personal reasons for remaining with the organization (e.g., tradition, comfort level, etc.) Collectively, these opportunities for team members to reflect and share become the impetus for moving otherwise stagnant team members into action.

I believe Maya Angelou's assessment that people will remember how we make them feel. Leadership title or no, we each have the power to make or break another's experience, but more so when we hold places of official authority.

PRACTICE HUMILITY

None of us is perfect. Some leaders may feel they must act through a flawless façade of omniscient perfection. Attempting to appear near perfect is a mistake that will more often than not alienate team members and erode trust that has, presumably, been nurtured as part of an exceptional work culture. Conversely, when leaders are humble, teams feel more connected and more appreciated.

To create a global culture, we must continuously check our collective biases regarding the ways in which strength, fortitude, and leadership must present. Until now, we've largely recognized character traits such as smugness, overconfidence, and hubris as indicators of leadership potential. But as the workforce evolves, so must our concept of what constitutes effective governance.

SERVE RELENTLESSLY

Leadership done well can be extremely exhausting because true leadership will always entail at least two distinct yet intertwined roles. The first role of leadership is to care for one's followers. The well-being of our teams becomes our responsibility. The secondary role is the actual achievement of organizational goals and objectives. I imagine there are some leaders reading this text and cringing at the thought of putting people ahead of processes and profit. However, I promise you, when humans feel seen, understood, and cared for, they unleash a type of energy, loyalty, and determination that will sustain your organization and have customers praising their experiences.

By now you've probably gathered that my approach to leadership is not always popular. When I consider the leadership styles we've explored in this chapter, I can honestly say that I have employed each style at times when they seemed the best, most expedient option. However, at my core I always return to the basics of serving and supporting my team.

DREAM TOGETHER

The best way I've found to elicit the innermost thoughts and best ideas from team members is to create an environment where they are compelled to share. Unrestricted by the threat of ridicule or censure, teams will expand the horizons of even the most visionary leader. How does one create such an environment? By first showing vulnerability and second ensuring the psychological safety of each team member throughout every idea exchange. As a leader, never be too proud or too stubborn to pivot. Thinking creatively and fearlessly means not being beholden to what has gone before. The perfect companion to the question *WHY* is naturally *WHY NOT*.

KEEP LEARNING

Many in the doctoral-bearing community joke that terminal degrees are referred to as such because by pursuing them, the actual intent is to kill you. Although it sometimes felt that way, the end result has been worth the trauma. One of the most important revelations I received resulting from doctoral studies was the recognition of what truly comprises knowledge and how little we all actually possess. Luckily for me—for all of us, really—lifelong learning is possible and in fact highly recommended.

In addition to traditional methods of acquiring new information, we may now choose between podcasts, webinars, and virtual conferences. Books, refereed journals, executive certification programs, in-person conferences, trade shows, and retreats are also enjoyable ways to remain abreast of new information, especially within one's primary industry or vocation. Encourage employees to report out new knowledge and findings to the team and show sincere gratitude for what you learn from these interactions. Consider partnering with a local library to host voluntary book clubs. Express an expectation of continuous learning and demonstrate that behavior for the team.

Well, there's the eight North Star rules. I thank you for accompanying me on a literary excursion along my heavily weeded leadership journey. This is the point where I get extremely transparent and confess that I have at times paid dearly for the privilege of staying true to my leadership convictions. Under the guidance of great CEOs, Vice Presidents, and Deans I have most often been gifted the opportunity to lead as I saw fit, enjoying amazing results in joy-filled cultures and exceeding institutional goals in the process. However, there have been a few times throughout my career where I have suffered at the hands of seemingly incompetent, insecure, vision-deprived supervisors; and I've struggled with choosing between abandoning my personal leadership style or enduring incessant workplace bullying and harassment from my more autocratic, Theory X (generally believes the worst about employees) superiors. Once I was even dismissed for refusing to compromise my core values and remaining true to my team as described throughout my eight leadership tenets.

Great leaders are not all extroverts! Introverts are leaders too! There should be more discussion in the world and guidebooks for how to effectively lead as an introvert. My greatest introverted strengths and attributes directly correlate to my service leadership style. I am thankful for a spot in this work because I want you to know that you are not alone, it can be done, and it takes all types of people to lead successfully.

And finally, step nine in my leadership recommendation is to consolidate a list of letters, notes, and cards of appreciation you have received over the years. Whenever you feel unappreciated, stressed out, or need a bit of external pick-me-up, review your list. This practice will help you tune into your inner voice and remind you of the great things you have achieved.

My Example of statements from supervisors, team members, and other colleagues:

- Thank you for your genuine and transparent approach to leadership.
- Most of all, thank you for creating a supportive and nurturing environment for our team.
- Thank you for pushing me to be my best and most professional self.
- Your dedication and vision continue to guide us in a stronger direction.
- Thank you for your constant support, encouragement, and joyful spirit that you bring to work every day.
- You are truly a light and positive role model, and I am honored to get to work with you.
- Thank you for coming to work [here] and making all our lives better.
- It's a joy working with you and dreaming of what could be—oh the possibilities. I look forward to another year of discovery and realizing dreams!
- We are fortunate to have your vision and leadership.
- Where do I start? Thank you for being my "rock" while I've been temping here the last three weeks. Seriously, I don't know what I

would have done without your continuous help!!

- Thank you for being such an intent listener.
- You're the kind of person I aspire to be and I am so grateful the universe allowed us to cross paths.
- Thank you so much for all that you do; for believing in me and advocating for me.
- Thank you for always allowing me to be myself.
- This is an invaluable gift—a masterclass in leadership and development.
- I truly enjoyed coming to work every day knowing that you would be there to provide leadership that guided our team in the right direction—and with laughs that helped us through the process.

INTRODUCING NATALIE BENAMOU

Natalie Benamou, MBA, accelerated her career to leadership positions in both the trade-show industry and non-profits. She has a *serve first* approach to life and leadership. She has held executive board director positions, been an advisor and mentor to women leaders, and served as president of nonprofit boards.

Turning her passion to action, Natalie is the Founder and CEO of HerCsuite® Leadership Programs and Network. She is the President and Founder of the non-profit HER HEALTHX which brings together patients, caregivers, women leaders, payers, providers, and industry to create health equity for women.

Natalie has been called a rainmaker by her clients and she provides strategic business consultation to win business and negotiate incredible deals. She speaks routinely, serves as an emcee for large events, and is a serial podcast host with over two-hundred interviews.

Personal Approach:

> *"People will forget what you said,*
> *they will forget what you did, but they will*
> *never forget how you made them feel."*
> —**Maya Angelou**

BAM! PIVOT TO PURPOSE

It is not uncommon to define ourselves by our career success. For years I strived to reach the top and never felt I had arrived. I look back now and realize that being in the top one percent of my industry meant I had arrived but was too caught up in the race to see it. People looking for a quick fix or a shortcut often asked me how I did it—how did I achieve so much? They are always surprised to hear there is no shortcut to success. My answer to the golden-ticket question is *It takes hard work and persistence.*

In February 2008, I was on my way to a large medical conference in San Francisco for an important client. I didn't want to be away from my two young daughters. I dreaded this trip and tears streamed down my cheeks as I drove to the airport. I knew the client was not happy with a corporate decision to increase their rates and I knew there was a challenging conversation awaiting my arrival.

After boarding the plane and settling in my seat, I

bent over to grab a book from my briefcase. I was looking forward to reading *Remember Me?* by Sophie Kinsella about a woman struggling with amnesia.

Bam! Everything went dark.

I reached behind my head and probed a tender spot on the back of my throbbing skull. I winced in pain and looked next to me and saw a small child. Bewildered, not knowing what had happened, I thought *I am glad whatever hit me, didn't hit that child.*

Stunned and seeing stars I called my husband.

"I don't feel so good," I hesitated and looked around. "I just got hit on the back of my head by someone's laptop bag."

Not fully understanding, he replied, "Take your neck pillow out and use it on the flight."

I looked up, confused, my vision swimming.

"Are you alright?" a kind flight attendant asked. *What is she asking me? Why aren't my words coming out right?*

"I don't know," I stammered, blinking back more tears as a sharp pang shot through my head. My neck was stiff, and I couldn't form words. I knew I was hurt.

"I don't feel well," I slurred. "I think I need to get off the plane."

Paramedics came, checked me out, and guided me up the jet bridge.

The lightning bolt of pain was more severe than a migraine, the concussion was real, and my life was transformed forever. That fifteen-pound laptop changed the trajectory of my life, and like the main character in the book I had planned to read on the plane, my brain would not work the way it had before.

The sudden traumatic brain injury caused me to lose life's moments, and the photographic memory I took for granted disappeared. Minutes, months, and years evaporated that instant. I wrestled to find the right words, and constant vertigo prevented me from the smallest activity including riding in a car.

Although I had a supportive team, I didn't have advisors who understood what I was experiencing and could give me critical career advice. Navigating career decisions is tough under the best of circumstances and I made the decision to leave my successful position and go to another company during one of the worst economic downturns in recent memory. I had to tap into resilience and grit to make my new path.

Two years later, I was at a women's group, and shared with a friend that my goal for the coming year was to expand my network. That friend invited me to attend the kick-off program for the Healthcare Businesswomen's Association (HBA) Chicago chapter. Although I wasn't feeling confident, I pushed past my fear, and I went to the event. There I was, still not fully recovered from my brain injury, unable to remember names, but I was meeting new people despite my challenges.

Before attending that event, my vision of the future was to recoup my career in the trade-show industry. I hadn't imagined the leadership transformation I was about to experience. What had started as a need to be surrounded by inspirational women resulted in an incredible personal and professional enlightenment.

When I walked into the impressive venue, I was greeted at the entrance and escorted to the registration table. I thought to myself, how warm and welcoming everyone was at this event. I was ushered toward and introduced to a group of strangers. Those small moments of being cared for and shepherded through registration and introductions were pivotal to me. I knew I had found the type of people I wanted to surround myself with.

I listened to the new HBA President, and the accomplished panel that evening and knew I was home.

As a leader, one of the most important things you can do is listen to your intuition. I knew this was the place for me and I joined HBA that evening and signed up as a volunteer for the membership committee.

LEADING LEADERS LESSON 1: DON'T WAIT UNTIL YOU ARE READY.

Volunteer, take action, and learn along the way.

If you have been waiting for the right moment, I am here to tell you there is no perfect moment, but life opens doors and shows us new opportunities. This time the path I chose turned out to guide me through my personal and professional life for the next thirteen years. Even though I was scared and did not feel like I was back to my fully capable self, I followed my intuition.

Six months after joining the Chicago chapter, I received a call from the chapter Past-President. She wanted me to consider filling an open board position. I hesitated carrying the weight of my memory loss and not being at my full strength. I forged ahead anyway.

I was invited to the President's home to attend the mid-year board retreat and to discuss the board position. As I drove to her house, I replayed this quote from Eleanor Roosevelt in my head: *"Do Something that Scares You Every Day."*

I was nervous, my confidence was low, and I knew I did not have the same networking capabilities I had before my brain injury. *What if they knew about my brain injury? What if they did not think I could do it? Should I tell them?* Self-doubt, when left unchecked, turns into negative self-talk and can create imaginary obstacles to success.

Determined to make a positive impression, I prepared well and researched everyone on the board in advance. I practiced remembering names on the drive that day, using all the tools in my toolbox to overcome the memory loss issues.

The board retreat went well, and I was voted in that day to the executive board. Suddenly, I was in!

The key to taking a new leadership role is to roll up your sleeves and put in the work. I became involved and volunteered consistently. It so happened that a few years later the chapter was struggling with a decrease in attendance at their monthly events. The board looked for ways to increase participation and monthly attendance because that was the primary source of new members. As an event professional, I knew how to deliver programs. Even though I had an Executive Board role as Board Secretary, I raised my hand and took on the added role of Interim Director-at-Large Programs.

"If you pull this off, I will nominate you for next year's President-Elect position," the current chapter President told me.

I worked closely with the programs team, and we created events that drew in attendees and increased membership. Inspired and empowered to make a difference and increase the opportunities coming my way, I went all in.

The first program was a powerful panel to talk about the Affordable Care Act (ACA) with Senior Executive Leaders, including a woman leader who is currently Chief Customer Officer at a major pharmaceutical company. We built momentum and delivered powerful programs that elevated women leaders in healthcare. Attendance increased and new members were rolling in.

True to her word, the President nominated me to be President-Elect. Four years after attending that first January event, I became President of the HBA Chicago Chapter. I was honored to lead a nineteen-person board and the eight-hundred-and-fifty-member organization. Through this leadership role I discovered my ultimate passion and calling—to lift-up and celebrate women— but it would take more learning before I put everything into action.

One of the greatest gifts happened the January after my term as President had concluded. At the end of a program where I spoke on a panel about confidence, an HBA member came up to talk with me. She mentioned a blog post I wrote while being President the year before. I listened in amazement as she shared with me how she had been living overseas and that blog post so inspired her that she printed it and hung it at her desk. It served as a constant reminder of her community of women back home.

In that moment I realized I had made a difference in her life. I was honored and moved. We have seen each other over the years; and every time, I am reminded of the difference I can make in the world—even with a brain injury. I *could* do this; in fact I *was* doing it. My new path paved; I was a leader with different capabilities than I had before, but still leading, nonetheless.

The decision I made to expand my network opened the doors to meaningful relationships and positions that impacted the rest of my life and career.

Ready to Stand Out?

As a leader, it is important to add value and find ways that help others gain visibility. Helping my clients move forward in their careers is something that comes naturally to me. In my role as Division Vice President for a trade-show company, I created all the sales revenue and directed the client relationships for the Chicago Division. Since I was the founder of the division, I felt a strong responsibility to the team and to our customers.

One of our largest clients had strict guidelines as part

of their master service agreement. Every year we had to demonstrate to procurement that we were saving money for their trade show program. After a certain point there aren't any more corners to cut to reduce costs and still deliver the desired result.

Most exhibit companies would have taken the cost reduction route for another year. After all, it was what the client was asking the company to do. That is a red ocean mindset, and it didn't serve the client nor the business. An alternative was to create something unexpected in a blue ocean.

I looked at all the fixed and variable costs including logistics, shipping, drayage, installation and dismantling. There were hidden costs including agencies spending time to make different sized graphics for every event, and meetings of thirty people to review different properties. I knew there was another way to deliver something unexpected. Taking a step back and looking at the broader landscape I found a solution, but it required a capital investment and a temporary increase in the budget.

I met with my team and proposed a novel idea: an increase in one-time spending to reduce long-term costs. It was radical but it was a financial win for both the organization and the client. Moving forward required a multi-step approach to achieving the desired outcome.

Whenever you are creating a solution, the individual who owns the budget is the key stakeholder for final approvals. In this case, our primary client contact was responsible for a multi-million-dollar program; however, she did not own the budget. This was not uncommon for a rising leader to have accountability but no financial authority. My aim was to help her secure the additional funds to ultimately save her company money.

LEADING LEADERS LESSON 2: WIN STAKEHOLDER BUY-IN.

Make a plan, secure support and be ready to adapt.

We needed a blue ocean strategy to create something unexpected and help differentiate ourselves and the client. When we were done, we had a ten-step strategy that led to measurable results and would prove to be profitable for years to come. We expanded our team, increased revenues, the client was promoted, and they reduced costs. Here is how we did it and this strategy can be applied to any scenario that requires a layered approval process.

The 10-Step Blueprint to Win Stakeholder Buy-In and Get Noticed

1. **Build Relationships**

   For this project, I had an insider advantage, which is something people often overlook. Having connections wide and deep in an organization will lead to greater opportunities, whether it is for a promotion or an adoption of a bold new idea.

   In this scenario, I had been working with this client for decades and was connected at every level throughout the organization all the way to the C-suite. I had coffee meetings, lunches and worked in the hallway to pre-sell ideas when leaders passed by. It ended up serving us as well. Our plan relied on enlisting internal allies to sway stakeholders who were initially skeptical to agree to this disruptive idea of spending more to save money. **Power Tip 1:** Whom do you need to align with before embarking on a new plan? Invite them to coffee and start creating relationships.

2. **Understand Priorities**

   To move an idea forward as a leader, understanding what matters most to each decision maker and the landscape of the budget is critical to a successful outcome. In this example, there were multiple product categories, and each leader had their own budget and idea of what success looked like. **Power Tip 2:** Ask questions, listen, and align your solution to their goals as the key to success.

3. **Develop a Compelling Case**

   We knew that to reach consensus, our client needed to be armed with an attractive solution. Since she didn't own the budget, the proposal had to win over the toughest leader with benefits for their brand. **Power Tip 3:** Be prepared with options, have a Plan B and C and be ready to answer questions.

4. **Communicate Benefits**

   Our client also needed to know every reason that this idea would be the right choice for each stakeholder and the company. We created slide decks that showed how the modular structure managed their entire trade show program and gave a consistent brand image. When preparing your presentation use a straightforward format. **Power Tip 4:** Make it easy for the decision maker to understand what they are getting in return for their investment, and how they personally will be seen as a visionary to their colleagues and the organization.

5. **Communicate the Plan**
   Since reducing cost was the inspiration for this project, it was important to show clean visuals and provide the context for the idea. In this scenario, it required taking every brand's requirement and demonstrating how a modular approach not only improved the bottom line, but also would enhance their visibility on the trade show floor.

   Create a plan with different levels of detail. Executive leaders want a short summary of the information, while mid-level leaders need to go deeper. **Power Tip 5:** Create a presentation that has layers, making it easy for you to adapt to the audience and win their trust.

6. **Highlight Risks of Status Quo**
   What happens if you do nothing? That was the compelling rationale to move forward. The company would continue to spend millions of dollars and their costs would spiral upward with the current approach to their event management program. The best way to mitigate the rising costs was to move forward with

an alternative plan. **Power Tip 6:** Share a do-nothing discussion to help leaders see the risk and be receptive to an alternative solution.

7. **Involve Others**
    If there are multiple stakeholders, each with their own goals and budget control, it is important to always be working on building consensus. In this case, we purposefully rolled out the material in a specific order to key stakeholders and supporters first; then built momentum as we moved forward sharing with other leaders.

    In addition to formal presentations, we held individual conversations that preceded the group meetings. The key decision makers felt included in the process and decision making while not being overburdened with details. **Power Tip 7:** Identify at the onset who will be your cheerleaders behind closed doors and engage them from the beginning.

8. **Explain the Benefits**
    It is easy to start with visually appealing presentations and overlook financials. In this case, the company would break even in the second year and realize

a decrease in spending in the third year. Start with how the solution benefits the bottom line to the organization. **Power Tip 8:** Create a long-range plan that shows the return on investment and how your proposal will achieve key performance metrics.

9. **Demonstrate Expertise**

   Leaders will move forward with someone they know, like, and trust. During the process, we gave our client ways she could share expertise with budgets, branding, and even elevated her with all the agencies who then shared with her leadership how effective she was executing this project. **Power Tip 9:** Leverage your knowledge outside of the project scope so that stakeholders see you as a thought leader before you ask for their support.

10. **Listen and Adapt**

    Not all projects get approved the first time around. It takes a careful plan and deliberate steps to reach the desired outcome. Along the way, be ready to adjust and adapt the plan based on feedback or inbound information. **Power Tip 10:** Listen and be ready with alternative solutions to keep the project moving forward.

CREATE A ROADSHOW

During the process, there was one leader who was not convinced about consolidating the exhibit program. He owned half of the annual budget and relied heavily on his agencies. We knew this and in addition to meeting with all the internal stakeholders, meetings were held with every agency to show how they would benefit from this concept. When it came to the final decision, everyone was on board and this final stakeholder gave his approval.

Road Show Tip: Win over leaders outside of the division and raise enthusiasm about the solution, even if it doesn't directly impact them. It creates camaraderie that will serve you on future projects.

CELEBRATE THE OUTCOME

This process elevated our primary client contact to gain visibility and be viewed as a strategic partner to the brand instead of someone who only executed programs. She was recognized for the success of the program and got promoted. We submitted the program for a coveted business award, the Stevie Award, and the company won an award for the rebranding project. Last but not least, agencies had new opportunities by creating interactive immersive experiences and their businesses benefited.

Celebrate Tip: Don't move on until you and the team experience the joy of success.

WHAT'S NEXT?

We all have a pivotal leadership moment. It can hit us on the head, like a laptop, or happen gradually. For me, the final moment happened on January 9th, 2020. I planned and delivered the first ever in-person networking event for my company. I called it EmpowHer, inspired by my first podcast Rock Your Trade Show. There were fifty people attending this in-person networking and leadership event at our manufacturing facility where I worked in a suburb of Chicago.

The goal of this program was to bring women together where they could meet, engage, and learn from each other and feel inspired. Secondarily, the company hoped to create future leadership opportunities and new business.

Leading up to the event, I met with our team, and we carefully crafted touchstone encounters to ensure the best possible experience. The draw for attendees was access to five Senior Leaders who would speak in small group settings. I tapped into my HBA network, and our speakers included a CMO and four Vice Presidents who each had a specific topic that she would speak with participants about.

We wanted every touch point to surprise and delight attendees. From registration through the farewell, our goal was for each woman to feel valued and walk away feeling inspired, informed, and connected with amazing women.

Speakers were specifically aligned with participants. Badges were printed, branded signage was created, and we designed the event flow. The plan was to greet each guest and escort her when she arrived to receive a badge and take her to the networking area, like the experience at my first HBA meeting.

Even though the weather was freezing that January evening, our facility was filled with engaging conversations from Networking Bingo to Spin to Win prizes everyone had stories to share with each other.

I was blessed that evening. The five women leaders delivered incredible programs in small cohort settings and the attendees raved about the event and couldn't wait to attend another one. We curated the attendee experience and fostered the ability to interact and engage with the speakers. The idea of surrounding ourselves with the right people came to life.

Seeing the attendees move from room to room and experience the knowledge the speakers shared made a profound impact both on their careers and me personally. I knew that there were senior leaders in transition and making career decisions. Others were seeking to grow businesses and find new ways to connect and grow.

Without knowing it, the future was calling me to find ways to lift women up. Facilitating conversations not only between the attendees but also with the speakers came naturally and would foreshadow an incredible pivot to follow this path later in the year.

I was so excited after the event that I called one of the speakers, on our drive home. Bubbling with possibilities, we both shared how amazing it would be if we could do this for other women. Imagine the impact we could make!

The rest of the year was a time like no other. After leading my division and transforming the company into a digital experiential organization, I made the decision to follow the dreams outlined after the event all those months earlier.

Inspired by the experience that evening, I felt my heart sing to lift women up. At the end of 2020, I launched HerPower2, Inc. and eventually HerCsuite® Network. Just like those small cohorts of women in January, we started with eleven of us coming together to meet, engage and thrive in meaningful ways.

What if we embrace messages like the one, I had on a cold night in January and take a leap of faith? Without realizing it, that evening served as the catalyst for the

HerCsuite® member experience. Women gaining access to thought leaders, getting advice they needed in the moment. Finding their next opportunity, networking, and feeling valued. Seeing women get promoted, find like-minded people, and know they are not alone is an honor.

Through the darkest moments of that year, the light was shining through the windows. The outcome was better than I could have ever imagined. I am living my purpose by celebrating and connecting women. It is easy to look back and think about all the steps we took to arrive.

When we feel unsure about what the future holds, it is an opportunity to listen to our hearts. Look up to the sky and dream of what can be, then make it so. I found my purpose through these leading leader moments. I know now that I am meant to lift women up, which I found through my years with HBA after getting a traumatic brain injury. I never would have realized this and made the life changing pivot to become an entrepreneur were it not for all the leadership lessons stacked up in my long career.

LEADING LEADERS LESSON 3: EXPRESS GRATITUDE

Be thankful to friends, colleagues, and your team. Let them know they matter.

I am so grateful to the friends who attended the event on January 9th, 2020, speakers who shared their knowledge and became founding members of HerCsuite® and for the many leaders along the journey who have supported and enabled me to advance women at every career stage—Thank you.

Doors close. Windows open. You get hit on the head. Embrace those moments. If there is one lesson, we have learned these past years it is life is short. Don't wait until you are ready, move forward anyway you can. Stand out by doing something unconventional and win stakeholder buy-in. As life gives you lessons, even when the road is difficult, take a moment to acknowledge them and express gratitude. Be thankful to those around you and to yourself.

Only you can summon the courage to take a step towards leadership. It is your courage that will empower you to move forward and persist. When you are faced with a choice, listen to the messages your heart is telling you. Open yourself up to the possibilities and embrace all that you are meant to be.

Keep shining your light bright. The world needs you.

INTRODUCING
M.L. "CISSY" PETTY

Dr. M.L. "Cissy" Petty is an experienced executive leader in higher education. She also serves as a conscientious leadership coach and consultant. Cissy leads with expertise, authenticity, curiosity, and confidence. She consults around the culture of work, leadership vulnerability, owning mistakes, and accepting achievements equally. Cissy has a keen understanding and experience with strategic planning, including organizational realignment, talent identification, and creating diverse and inclusive teams. Most importantly, she stresses the capacity to create and build a strong foundation for engagement that values connectedness and belonging.

For over thirty years, at four different universities, Cissy served as the Vice President for Student Affairs and Dean of Students. University members describe her as having high energy, a drive to accomplish bold projects and a keen eye for details. Her students describe her as "a lightning bolt on two feet." She describes herself as a change agent, a relentless advocate for learning, and a person comfortable with seeing the potential in people, places, and things. She believes deeply that learning opens the possibilities to reimagine what can happen at any given moment.

Cissy has a Ph.D. in Higher Education, Florida State University. She was selected for the prestigious postdoctoral fellowship, Upsilon Nu Chi Distinguished Scholar in counseling, University of North Carolina Greensboro. Her background education also includes Harvard University Senior Institute for Higher Education Management; Nationally Certified Counselor; Board Certified Coach; Executive Leadership Coaching Certification, Georgetown University; and she completed a two-year certificate course in Spiritual Studies, St. Thomas University. Cissy is recognized nationally for her leadership, receiving the National Association of Student Personnel Administrators Pillar of the Profession and the Florida State University Distinguished Alumna in the College of Education.

AUTHENTIC LEADERSHIP: TRUST AND GRACE IN ACTION

"Great teams do not hold back with one another.
They are unafraid to air their dirty laundry.
They admit their mistakes, their weaknesses,
and their concerns without fear of reprisal."
—Patrick Lencioni [1]

Discovering how to navigate a staff, an organization, and its leadership structure is no easy task. There are thousands, probably millions, of articles, books, and webinars about the researched topic of leadership. There are three vital parts of leadership: authenticity, trust, and grace.

---

1   Lencioni, Patrick, The Five Dysfunctions of a Team (Jossey-Bass, 2002) 44.

Leading is a complex skill and no two people approach it the same way. While there are no perfect leaders, learning how to be a leader is a daily practice. While most leaders strive to do their best, all leaders make mistakes. The difference between success and failure is a leader who is always striving to improve. This is how authenticity, trust, and grace are woven into leadership practice.

Over the course of a leader's tenure, they sometimes fail their teams and themselves. As a leader, I have missed the mark, misunderstood others, and made other mistakes. Authentic leaders recognize that being fully human means holding success and failure equally. Everyone watches and evaluates the person who holds the leadership title. In an organization, there are people who want you to succeed and others who hope you fail. Daniel Pink writes, *"Authenticity requires boldness. And when authenticity is thwarted so is growth. The most telling demonstration of this point came from several dozen people from all over the world who describe their regret—their failure to be bold—with the same five words: 'Not being true to myself.'"* [2] How you navigate both wins and losses are the keys to authenticity, trust, and grace in action.

---

2   Pink, Daniel, Power of Regret, Riverbend Books, NY, 2008, pg. 109

The leaders I admired most were those who accepted that they were flawed. When they failed at delivering a project, they owned it, and worked diligently to rectify the situation, with no excuses. If they blew their cool under pressure, they apologized to the individual, as well as publicly and promised they could and would do better. Perhaps one of the greatest teachable moments a leader has is her recognition of failing. Falling short or not measuring up teaches us lessons in humility, restores grace, and develops integrity. No one is infallible, as failures and mistakes happen to leaders and team members alike. Parker Palmer, in his book, *Let Your Life Speak*, writes "*My life is not only about strengths and virtues; it is also about my liabilities and limits, my trespass and my shadow.*"[3] Further, Palmer encourages us to embrace *"what we find shameful about ourselves as well as what we are confident and proud of."* [3] This is the wholeness good leaders seek to embrace. A leader's authenticity is a measure of her humanity. A lesson I learned recently involved a staff member, who delivered news that what was promised to an executive leader was not going to happen. A jolt of adrenaline shot through me—fear of failure, fear of the executive's reaction, fear of disappointing students. To state I overreacted

3   Palmer, Parker. Let Your Life Speak, Listening to the Voice of Vocation. Jossey-Bass, Inc. 2000, pgs. 6-7

would be an understatement. I embarrassed myself, and a staff member who was talented. While I apologized, it still did not seem sufficient. I used the story publicly to remind myself of, and to offer to others, the gift of redemption when owning failure.

Susan Scott, author of *Fierce Leadership,* shares *"One of the greatest challenges we all face is understanding and embracing our own leadership potential. Even the most highly paid executives struggle with the internal questions about their personal effectiveness. This is normal. Our results, attitudes, beliefs, prejudices, fears, hopes, glories, and broken places have led us all to practices that others celebrate or question, that ourselves celebrate or question."*[4] Authentic leadership is built on the willingness to admit shortcomings. Leaders are "perfectly imperfect" and are not infallible when responding and handling every situation. The importance of hiring, training, and developing a team cannot be understated because the best solutions are achieved together.

The culture must be open, honest and complete conversations. In her book, *Wired for Authenticity,* Henna Inman shares, *"Authenticity is not deciding who you are and then rigidly applying this to every situation. Instead,*

---

4   Scott, Susan, "Fierce Leadership, A Bold Alternative to the Worst 'Bests,'" Practices of Business Today (Crown-Press, NY, 2009) 292.

authenticity is leading adaptively from your core, choosing who you need to be to serve the greatest good. We expect our leaders to show up at work perfectly rational employees. Instead, what we get are human beings."[5] Authentic leaders admit mistakes, and this provides opportunities for credibility and strengthens a team. The quickest way to achieve trust is to tell the truth and move forward. This is a powerful place for candidness, honesty, respect and deepening trust.

TRUST

Jack Welch, former CEO for General Electric defines trust as the following: "*I could give it a dictionary definition, but you know it when you feel it. Trust happens when leaders are transparent, candid, and keep their word. It's that simple.*"[6] I discovered this quote while participating in a workshop. I use Stephen M.R. Covey's practical work during retreats, workshops, and during coaching and consulting sessions. Through my own leadership growth, I learned trust can be repaired, restored, and grace bestowed.

Covey defines trust as both a noun and a verb which can have several meanings. In his book, *The Speed of*

---

5   Inman, Henna, Wired For Authenticity, Seven Principles to Inspire, Adapt and Lead. (www.tranforleaders.tv 2015) 29
6   Welch, Jack. Leading at the Speed of Trust Workbook, Franklin-Covey and Covey Link, LLC., 2008. Pg.1

Trust, he writes: "*Simply put, trust means confidence. When you trust people, you have confidence in them, their integrity and abilities.*"[7]

He also highlights the importance of restoring trust when broken. For work relationships to be whole it is necessary to correct misbehavior. "*Admit when you're wrong, apologize quickly, show it is necessary to right wrongs.*"[8] Covey goes on to write, "extend trust abundantly to those who have earned it, conditionally to those who are still earning it."[9]

As leaders, teams often measure leadership as a combination knowing what to do and having the skills to perform. Covey confirms in his work that "*trust is equal parts of character and competence.*"[10] Leadership and trust are inseparable. No leader or leadership style is one hundred percent effective in all scenarios. Leading teams requires leaders to understand that there are times when decisions are made that others do not agree with or understand. There also are occasions when there are poor actions on the part of the leader. When either of these two things

---

7   Covey, Stephen R. Free Press, Division of Simon Schuster, Inc. 2006. pg. 5.
8   Covey, Stephen R. Free Press, Division of Simon Schuster, Inc. 2006. pg. 160.
9   Covey, Stephen R. Free Press, Division of Simon Schuster, Inc. 2006, pg. 229.
10   Covey, Stephen R. Covey, Free Press, Division of Simon Schuster, Inc. 2006, pg. 32

occur, the leadership team's trust may falter. Authenticity, trust and grace offer the opportunity for the team to be restored.

Jeff Gorman, President of Keller Schroeder consultants, adds with depth:

"If you trust your teammate, even when they seem to have done something wrong, you will seek to understand why they did what you asked them not to do. Regardless of the person or their role, you would work to understand intention before you passed judgement. Two things can happen in this kind of scenario when you trust, extend grace, and seek to understand. First, you could find out that indeed there were legitimate reasons for things to change. In this case, you grow the foundation of trust with the teammates by demonstrating that you did not have the default assumption they were deliberately doing things against your direction. You can work together, and even have healthy conflict, based on the legitimacy of their course of action. Second, you could find out it was a true mistake. In this case, you still exhibited a foundation of trust by seeking to understand before passing judgement. Extending grace to build and demonstrate trust within the team is about having the perfect balance

between empathy and accountability; it is resisting the temptation to assume the intention of others. It is about being able to care enough about others to hold them accountable while making them know they are valued as a person."[11]

The gift of offering trust and restoring trust when broken is valuable beyond measure. Trust is a vital source for achieving not simply success, but a shared vision realized.

GRACE

Grace is not a word often used in describing leadership practices. A leader who successfully extends grace has a powerful tool in her leadership toolbox. Grace is given to pardon an offense and to show mercy. Shelia Murty, former Forbes Human Resources Council member, writes *"Grace is the act of creating an opening where you can see a life that is different than yours, and where you have empathy and compassion—an opening where people reveal more of themselves to you and feel safe to do so. We all need grace, and we need more of it now than ever."*[12] Failure and disappointment often opens your heart and leads to

---

11   Gorman, Jeff. Trust and Grace, keller-schroeder.com, October 10, 2020, pg.1

12   Murty, Shelia. What It Means to Lead with Grace, Forbes Human Resources Council Post, July 7, 2020

lessons of leadership that redirect your time, energy and responses to others.

Gibson and Schinoff, in their article, "The Little Things That Affect Our Work Relationships," write, "*We tend to think about relationships in the wrong way: we categorize them as either good or bad, and we think they will always stay the same. As a result, we don't try and fix the ones that have soured, and we take the healthy relationships for granted.*"[13] A dose of humility is a valuable partner with grace.

Humility helps us understand our own limitations and blind-spots and invites others to contribute in different and complementary ways.

I fell in love with the word "grace" because I knew deeply that I needed it. I also knew at my core, that I needed to extend it to others. Like all relationships, friends, family, and colleagues we have expectations that go unmet. We react and our reactions can be powerful in a variety of ways that we alone cannot measure. My reactions typically came from the fear of disappointing others. If I failed to meet a deadline, or if I failed to be prepared for a meeting, I was disappointed with myself. That said, my reaction rolled like a wave to those around

---

13   Gibson, Kerry Roberts and Schinoff, Ben. "The Little Things That Affect Our Work Relationships," Harvard Business Review. May 29, 2019, pg.1

me. Looking back, I wish I had more courage to simply own it and say "I'm sorry" more quickly.

Following up with team members, individually or in a meeting is good practice. It can add valuable perspective. Especially during stressful times, it is important to gauge wellbeing. Look for opportunities to connect when they present themselves. We owe it to our teams, collectively and individually, to check-in on the ebb and flow of our work relationships. Making time for one another provides an opportunity to offer grace and restore trust as necessary.

We have inherited leadership models that are antiquated, and yet many institutions, businesses, and organizations still use the "tried and not so true anymore" model of leadership. No longer do we need to subscribe to a model that simply prescribes what employees do, what silos are created, or the competition for recognition or resources. While we are not quite there yet, many leaders have begun efforts to shrink "fiefdoms" by sharing and collaborating with others across the organization. One such leader is Antonio (Tony) Castillo, the founder and managing partner of Vigilant Training Group, LLC. Tony was a guest presenter at the Supply Chain Leaders in Action (SLCA) Executive Think Tank. Amy Thorn, from SLCA, shared the following, "*Tony shows how great communication and collaboration are bound together with grace. Trust is the foundation of any relationship. If you don't have trust, it's tough to do anything. Without it nothing can be built. He used a simple acronym using the letters to spell out grace: G-Generosity, R-Respect, A-Action, C-Compassion, E-Energy.*"[14]

Authentic leadership is built on the willingness for leaders to admit shortcomings. No leader responds adequately in all situations, but she knows when the team works together, the outcomes are better. The leader is responsible for hiring, training, and trusting her team. The culture of the organization, established by leadership, must allow the leader and the team to have full, honest, open, and sometimes robust conversations. No one likes to fail; owning a mistake establishes credibility and strengthens the team. The quickest way back to trust is telling the truth and moving forward. This is a powerful place for grace given and received.

Grace is the glue and is the key to building, extending, and restoring authentic relationships. Leading provides daily lessons for both the leader and the team. The lessons revolve around understanding the practices and the

---

14   Thorn, Amy. Grace: A Key Aspect of Leadership You May Not Have Considered. SLCA, https: www.slcasupplychain.com, October 10, 2020.

principles of integrity, courage, reflection, and forgiveness. These lessons have the capacity to restore trust and clearly demonstrate grace in action.

1. AUTHENTIC LEADERSHIP: TRUST AND GRACE ACTION PLAN FOR LEADERS

Self-awareness and self-development are critical while you simultaneously develop the team. Commit and model for the team ways you are aligning your "walk" with your "talk." Participate in staff development workshops, get certified in an area of leadership that inspires you, be an avid reader and share resources with others. Consider a leadership coach. Review what you learn about yourself with a trusted colleague, partner, or friend. Think about what it means to own your story—the good and the bad. Learn about your worst behaviors or tendencies you might portray under stress, and watch for them. No matter how seasoned you are as a leader you are always growing and improving. This is the lesson of being fully human.

2. LEADING IS BOTH AN ART AND A SCIENCE.

Remind yourself and your team that leadership, like art and science, is often a grand and messy experiment. It is ok to make mistakes, and then "rewrite the script." Go ahead and have the hard conversation, give and accept the apology. Allow yourself to be vulnerable and accept whatever failure occurs as a learning opportunity. Remember that changed behavior goes a long way in restoring trust. Extend trust to the other person first, before simply expecting others to extend "positional" trust to you.

3. DO NOT BE AFRAID OF BEING WRONG.

Fear is not a good partner in team building or decision-making. Being wrong is an opportunity to include others in the decision-making process. Most people deeply respect the one who can admit her mistakes. Build a culture of grace within the organization. Both the leader and team members fall short at times. Be humble, no one has all the answers. It is important that we offer each other the motto: *We can and should do better.*

4. PRACTICE SEEING SITUATIONS FROM DIFFERENT VANTAGE POINTS.

Understand the strengths and the challenges you possess, and similarly those of your team. Use their collective and individual wisdom and perspectives in critical situations and decisions that can impact others. It is important to recognize that team members have opportunities to see issues at ground level. This is a great conduit of information. This practice is key in clarifying strategic plans and operational guidelines.

5. EMPOWER THOSE AROUND YOU.

The team must be free to do their best work. Be clear, supportive and offer the needed training. Consider building opportunities for the team to participate in leadership coaching. Let them know that you both admire and trust their work. Giving the team confidence and appropriate tools are skills worth exercising and a positive investment.

6. BUILD A COLLABORATIVE CULTURE.

Working together is paramount for team success. Ultimately, it is important that the team review and share the organization's values. Encourage members to voice support and concerns regarding potential incongruencies between policy and practice. It is also important for leadership to offer programs of interest, not necessarily pertinent to work, but important for health and well-being. It takes everyone to ensure that work is a safe and welcoming place.

7. BE A CURIOUS LEADER.

Do not be afraid to challenge the status quo. This is how change happens and new ways of working and leading emerge. Looking at what has always been done with new eyes can be a valued gift to the organization. Some may be challenged by novel thinking; but it is imperative that we seek new perspectives. Children often corner the market on being imaginative, wondering how things work, and how things come apart. If all of us could practice such childlike wonder, just imagine what we might discover anew.

8. WE ARE STRONGER TOGETHER.

Connection and belonging matter a great deal in fostering authenticity, trust and grace. Leaders must create climates that foster differing thoughts and opinions. In doing so, they free up opportunities to try new ways of looking at a project, new thoughts on team development, new ideas for gathering feedback, and simply ways to relax and have fun. All team members need to experience the sense of being valuable to the team and experience meaningful connections. No one ever owns success alone; success takes a team.

9. FORGIVE.

Forgiveness is often overlooked when discussing leadership. Every leader makes errors of judgement. It is important that the leader first owns the issue, and then begins the work of forgiving themselves. This opens the ability to extend the same grace to those on the team that will make similar mistakes. There is no shame when you try to do your best work. Forgiving yourself and others makes way for renewed effort, ideation, creativity and problem-solving. Being forgiven is a powerful feeling of redemption, adding depth to connection and belonging.

10. TAKE TIME FOR YOU.

It is important for leaders to take time for themselves. Choose what helps you relax: the beach, the movies, going out to dinner, reading, binge watching your favorite Netflix show, exercise, visiting with family and friends, etc. It does not really matter what you do, simply make sure your own time is scheduled. I know you may think you are too busy, but the truth is you get more done when you first take care of yourself. This also means the basics: sleeping well, eating healthy, exercising for stress relief, and journaling for reflection. You are worth the investment of time!

Find Your Purpose. Simon Sinek made *Start with Why* not just a great book to read, but its title is a statement, often repeated in both homes and offices. Your *why* is the cornerstone of what drives you. It is a combination of purpose and inspiration coming together. Your *why* includes the depth of your mind, body and spirit. It is not simply about a particular job, position, or duty. Your *why* can add to the body of knowledge. Your *why* has the capacity to enrich relationships and create something that makes life more purposeful.

11. REFLECT

One of the most important traits leaders possess is the ability to reflect on both their successes and failures. Reflection offers an opportunity to review and determine what went well and what did not. In his article, "Leadership Character: The Role of Reflection," author Eric Kail writes, "Reflection is what links our performance to our potential. It is the process of properly unpacking ourselves as leaders for the good of others."[15]

Self-reflection has the capacity to be a powerful teacher. At every level, leaders and staff have opportunities to create high performing teams. Authenticity, trust, and grace in action is a blueprint for creating a more successful leadership experience for all.

---

15   Kail, Eric "Leadership Character: The Role of Reflection." *The Washington Post*, June 10, 2011.

INTRODUCING
MYLENE BARIZO

Emigrating from Manila to Los Angeles as a child, Mylene Barizo never imagined a career in corporate America. Challenging cultural norms and family expectations, she rose to VP of Human Resources at Enterprise Holdings and served as the Senior Executive Director of HR to the CIO at The Boeing Company. Mylene led teams that innovated in the HR space while also building human capital strategies with senior executives and the C-suite. Go to www.leadership-ladder.com to find stories and lessons-learned in her *Recipes of Leadership* blog, to access her for executive coaching and speaking engagements, and to learn about the projects and organizations she's involved with that focus on diversity and elevating women and BIPOC (Black, Indigenous, People of Color) talent to their next levels of success.

A proud UCLA Bruin and former Los Angelena, Mylene now calls Seattle home. She's a doting auntie to Layni and Logan and loves sharing adventures with them. So don't be surprised if you bump into her at a restaurant in France, a cava bar in Spain, a theater production in England, or on a beach in Greece as she explores beautiful places on the planet, savors fabulous food, and builds memories with friends and loved ones!

RECIPES OF LEADERSHIP

I am. Two simple words that encompass so much, especially when descriptors and details are added. Those two words signal that an outline of a person's unique perspective is coming. It provides the framework for me to share what I am and who I have become.

In my case, I am a woman of color, an immigrant, and a title-carrier of multiple *firsts*: first generation, first grandchild of the first born on my mother's side, first to go to an American university, and the list goes on. Because I was a first, my Filipino-born-and-raised parents couldn't offer much guidance on certain things. Our experiences and frames of reference were so different. From college applications and into my professional career, these were processes I had to maneuver through on my own.

If my chosen career path was typical (or stereotypical) in my community—like being a nurse or medical doctor—then I could access friends or extended family members for guidance. They could provide insights and support around how to prepare for grad school, how to connect to mentors, and how to study for board exams. But that wasn't the path I chose.

I was the *first*. First to launch myself into a corporate career. And I had no idea what a corporate career looked like or what it even meant to climb a corporate ladder. It wasn't until after I accepted a job offer and was working in the trenches that I realized: I wanted to lead. It wasn't enough to be told that I had a natural propensity for leadership. I wanted responsibility. I wanted the title. I wanted the financial rewards. But not knowing how to get there, I had to figure out what "leadership" was along the way.

LEADERSHIP RECIPE

I love food! Recipes are a formula of sorts, but a flexible formula. While my mom's *pancit* (Filipino noodle dish with rice noodles / bean thread noodles / shredded chicken / and lots of veggies cooked in soy sauce and some chicken broth) was tasty, there are so many other versions of pancit that I love. Some have fat, udon-like noodles and a thicker, almost gravy-like sauce. Another version has noodles topped with shrimp, sliced hard-boiled eggs, and practically no veggies. They are all pancit—just in different and tasty forms.

If leadership is a tasty dish, what are the ingredients? How do I bring them all together to create my unique recipe? I needed to figure out what leadership looked like. I needed to learn what attracted me to some leaders and repelled me from others. Somewhere in that process I had to assess my own skills. What skills did I have? Which would help me become an effective leader? Without a guidebook—and choosing a career path that prompted bewildered looks and probably a fair amount of skepticism from my parents and family—my journey began.

I went to work for Enterprise Rent-A-Car after graduating from UCLA.

This was a bold move. A leap into the unknown. No one in our family chose the "corporate America" path. I didn't know anyone in a senior leadership position and don't think my parents or I ever thought about what it took to become an executive leader in a major corporation. When I shared my decision, I braced for pushback. To their credit, mom and dad said something along the lines of, "If you think this is the right opportunity for you, then we trust your judgment. Work hard and do your best." While their eyes were saying something closer to: *Really?! We sent you UCLA so you could rent cars for a living?!* I'm grateful that they gave me the space, trust, and support to find my way, even though the Management

Trainee job seemed to be basic retail with little opportunity for advancement.

First, I interviewed HR then with the Area Rental Manager and my eventual boss. Both intrigued me with themes like: we promote only from within based on performance rather than tenure; we provide a path to management and senior leadership; we work hard and play hard; we teach you how to run a business *and* your compensation will grow based on your performance and as the business grows. But it was the team at the Santa Clarita location that sealed the deal. Everyone was a lot like me. We were all college graduates, who liked to compete, and were fun, yet driven. There was a dynamic vibe in the office. I could see myself working with this team and having fun in the process.

Within the first month of my Enterprise career, I got my first impactful lesson in leadership.

It was Friday afternoon—a super busy time because cars rented early in the week were now all returning. It was hot—ninety-degrees outside—and when you put those two together, customers get grumpy with long waits and harried employees.

My teammates and I were running. Literally running. Running in full business attire—skirt, nylons, and heels for me—we ran back and forth from the rental counter to the parking lot helping customers return the cars and providing shuttle services.

At the height of the frenzied activity, a gentleman walked into our branch office. He was tall, in a nice suit and dress shoes, and wore a fancy watch. He looked around and removed his suit jacket. Loudly, he asked the customers in the lobby, "Who needs a ride back to a dealership or shop?" I immediately went to my manager, Jeff, and said, "Some guy is trying to steal our customers!" Jeff looked at the gentleman, looked back at me, and said, "Don't worry about it, just keep taking care of the customers." Okay: I guess Jeff knew this guy. If Jeff says we're good, I guess we're good.

It was after six-thirty that evening when things calmed down. All the customers were gone, and our lobby was quiet. Wrap-up duties—inventory review; counting cash for the deposit; vacuuming the office etc.—were about done when the well-dressed stranger approached me.

"Mylene," he said, "I wanted to welcome you to the team and introduce myself. I'm Greg Stubblefield—but everybody calls me Stubby. "I want to thank you for choosing to build your career at Enterprise. I know you're commuting thirty to forty-five minutes each way from the valley to here. I'm working on getting you transferred to an office closer to where you live so your commute won't be as long. We have long hours here and a long commute makes for an even longer day so I want you to know that we're working on this."

I sputtered out my thanks and thought to myself, *Who was this guy? And how did he know about me?*

Greg was the regional vice president for the San Fernando Valley, part of San Gabriel Valley, Ventura, Santa Barbara, and San Luis Obispo counties. He was my boss' boss' boss—and he knew my name! I saw him a few weeks later at a company-hosted Kings game; and again, he greeted me by name. I was hooked! I was in awe. Here was a man who held a senior level position and took the time to get to know a little about me, the newest of newbies. This was the first time I felt like I *knew* someone in a leadership role.

The moment ticked by, and I knew then and there that I wanted to be a leader. I wanted to be just like Stubby.

Meeting Stubby and experiencing his brand of leadership was the first time I became acutely aware of what leadership could look like. It opened my eyes to how the branch and area managers I worked for led me and our teams. I wish I could say that I was intentionally taking an inventory of my skills and comparing them to the leaders I admired. Nope. I wasn't that sophisticated, I was young. But there were skills and traits that drew me in and others that I knew I didn't like or caused me to lose respect for people. While I couldn't really name what my brain was processing, I began creating my personal recipe of leadership.

The gathering of ingredients for my recipe took off from there.

Stubby showed me that charisma, personal connectivity, and authenticity were leadership elements I valued. True to his word, in a few months I was transferred to the Woodland Hills branch—10 minutes from home. There I met my next teacher on this leadership journey. Bradley Robert Carr.

Bradley Robert Carr taught me the tactical elements of branch operations. He and the assistant manager pushed me to practice what I learned. I had to show them I could execute processes consistently and well. With Brad's guidance, nudging, and support I passed my MQI (management qualification interview—a requirement before you could be considered for a promotion to assistant manager) nine months into joining Enterprise.

Momentum was building. This was starting to look like a career! But the tactical knowledge and ability to execute weren't the only, or even most valuable, things Brad taught me. In fact, his impact on my career came after I *stopped* working directly for him.

In the six months after passing my MQI, both Brad and I got promoted, he to area manager of the West San Fernando Valley & East Ventura County and me to assistant branch manager of the Thousand Oaks location. I set out to improve fractured relationships with referral sources in my territory. Marketing, as we called it, seemed like fun. I was good at it. Relationship-building came easily to me.

On a regional level, a new role was created to build local corporate accounts. This foray into corporate rentals was a preparatory step to accessing the airport and business rental markets—a segment wherein Enterprise didn't really have a presence—as we diversified our customer base. I happened to mention to Brad that the new corporate account's role and program sounded super interesting. It sounded so exciting to be part of building a brand-new revenue stream for the company.

That seemingly minor comment started a chain reaction that changed the course of my career. I didn't realize that leadership ingredients were coming together to form a main dish. Unbeknownst to me, Brad started conversations with our regional vice president, Richard Thrasher. Brad spoke of my work ethic in Woodland Hills, how I repaired relationships in Thousand Oaks, the business growth that resulted from my efforts, and my interest in the corporate accounts program.

One day Richard randomly showed up at my branch. I was terrified. Why would my boss' boss' boss wanted to meet with me? He took me to lunch and shared that an opportunity to run the corporate accounts program for our region was on the horizon. The role reported directly to him. I would be part of the regional leadership team and among the first corporate account managers—the rumor was there were only twelve or so in the company— tasked with building out this new business line. Was I interested? If so, the job was mine.

This was the first time I experienced *advocacy*. While I didn't know to use that word back then, today I realize (and so appreciate) what Brad did. He put my name forward, endorsed me for this larger role, and leveraged his access to leadership on my behalf. This was advocacy in action.

Brad brought two additional ingredients for my leadership recipe. First, he challenged me to learn and grow. He worked from the assumption that I could do it—whatever "it" was. It didn't matter if I felt prepared. It didn't matter how little experience I had. He believed in my ability to grow into the challenge. Second, he spoke my name in circles I didn't have access to—circles that included other leaders and where decisions were made.

He attached his name and reputation to mine and opened doors to opportunities that I didn't know existed.

Brad gave me another important gift: the chance to work with Richard. Richard was my next teacher in leadership as our relationship spanned eighteen of my twenty-three years at Enterprise.

The first ingredient lesson Richard gave me was trust. The corporate accounts manager's role was an outside sales position. I was rarely in the office. He gave me complete autonomy. He trusted me to do my job. That's why it was so hard for me to tell him, after two years in the role, that I didn't see myself in outside sales for the rest of my career. I knew that if I wasn't having fun and my performance dropped, I would be let go. Enterprise required performance and accountability. I told him, "You trusted me with this opportunity, and I trust you with my career. If there's something else out there that you think I could be good at, let me know."

And that's how my transition into the HR function occurred. When Richard first mentioned becoming an HR generalist, I didn't just balk—I cried. Crying in front of my boss, I thought that he must hate me for giving me a desk job, pushing paper, and never seeing the light of day. The first of several lessons came from our conversation that day.

Richard reminded me that Enterprise is all about *building a business and making it your own.* With so many changes coming to what we knew as the personnel department, he challenged me to build the role into what I thought it should be. To create it. To own it. Then he empowered me to turn my ideas into reality—a new ingredient.

Empowerment. Another word I likely didn't know to use in my early career but experienced under Richard's leadership. The autonomy and support he gave me opened my mind and stretched my capabilities. It sparked my creativity and allowed me to initiate a variety of projects. I updated our regional intern program. I created training for first-line managers (how to transition from individual contributors to managers) and built branch-manager training modules (covering practical themes like compliance, policy reviews, and team building) at a time when development programs only existed for area rental managers.

Was it easy? No. I needed to sell my ideas to the regional leadership team. Not everyone felt great about taking managers away from their branches for training. Some saw my ideas as a cost—time away from the customer was lost revenue rather than an investment in our talent and our future. I was a one-woman department.

It took time to create the training, build the content and materials needed, and plan logistics for the event; I needed help and more ingredients for my leadership recipe. Not only was Rich a vocal supporter of my ideas, he invested resources and provided administrative head-count so I could execute on those ideas.

My business partnership with Richard evolved and grew as I followed him to Washington state in 2000. The move was a promotion (to a "group" level position—larger territory, more employees, and multiple business units) and an opportunity to lead my first HR team. Bumbling through learning how to lead a departmental team while also figuring out what to do in this new and larger role, was overwhelming at times. Thankfully, another leadership teacher with her own ingredients would soon be thrown into the pot.

The Enterprise culture put a lot of emphasis on the people. The mission statement establishes our people and customers as equal, top priorities. I saw many forms of that people-first mentality with Stubby, Bradley Robert Carr, and Richard. But Ms. Chris Cummings taught me two more dimensions: embracing the teammate wholely as a person and the power of developing your team. Her insights added new ingredients and a flavorful depth to my leadership recipe.

As a wife, mom of two, and our senior finance leader, Ms. Chris opened my eyes to the facets of life that come with each teammate. I chose not to have children, and I was ignorant when it came to what it took to manage a family, a home, and a career. Even though both my parents worked, I didn't realize how insensitive I was to the demands that came with trying to balance work and family.

I watched Ms. Chris make it a priority to be at her girls' school events, support new moms at Enterprise, and heard her impress on everyone that the business would be fine and to go take care of their family. I learned the importance of looking beyond the individual who showed up to complete the tasks at the company. From fur babies, bucket list travel plans, celebrating personal and professional milestones moments, all the way to providing pep talks when things got hard, Ms. Chris embraced everything that came with each person. She showed me that a supported teammate was a happy, productive, and loyal teammate.

Her efforts didn't stop there. Ms. Chris's second key ingredient was developing her people. The greater lesson was *how* she developed them. It didn't matter what you did within the business—B2B sales, daily rental operations, finance, HR—she spoke the language of your space.

Hearing her code-switch from assessing financial risks of fleet customers, to building market share in the rental segment, to improving culture in a functional department; listening to her was fascinating. Inspiring. Ms. Chris was all about teaching others how to be businesspeople. While our chats were rarely called formal training or mentoring sessions, it wasn't unusual for a conversation to start with personal stories and end with a professional development goal. Sharing stories of my last vacation evolved into a discussion about promotional opportunities and how to set goals.

Ms. Chris taught me, and others, how to start with the end in mind. Begin with the business in mind and key deliverables. Then figure out how your space contributes to those goals. Next, create and build the systems needed to strategically execute on both my goals and the business deliverables. Not only was she consistent in her message, but she also followed up. She held us accountable. She drove the leadership team to work in collaboration with each other. And she helped us find opportunities to strengthen those skills. She reinforced and elevated themes and ingredients I took from Richard: *you can't do it all*, *you need to teach your people*, *trust your team*. Finally, she reminded me that when you strengthen one, you strengthen the whole. She was the personification of advice Richard shared with me long ago: *leadership is about everybody but you.* Ms. Chris made our leadership team better and added richness to my leadership recipe.

Over fifteen years my leadership recipe took shape. It started with learning the power of charisma and authenticity that Stubby exuded. Bradley Robert Carr taught me business operations while also gifting me with advocacy. Richard taught me about leading from a place of trust and showed me what empowerment looked and felt like. And Ms. Chris opened my eyes to embracing the whole person, the value of learning other business languages, and the power that comes with developing a team. What came next? Putting those recipe components together to create my own flavor of leadership.

As a new leader I naively thought that as long as I used these ingredients, all would be well. My team—any team—would follow. We would have fun. We would produce. We would lead other teams. But the lesson I learned was, just bringing the components of the recipe together wasn't enough. Salt might be a key ingredient, but too much will destroy a dish. I had to learn proportions. I had to learn balance. I had to understand how to adjust ingredients in my leadership recipe based on the situations I was in and audiences I addressed. It was time *to learn from those I was responsible for leading.*

Jenn taught me the importance of connecting my goals and deliverables to the goals I set for the team. Mike taught me that my-way-or-the-highway isn't a great approach to building trust. Janine taught me that everyone articulates a problem or project differently; listening and patience are key. Laura taught me that focusing more on the cost of a teammate rather than the value they bring will likely prompt them to leave for another opportunity. No matter how fun the workplace was, how much I thought I empowered people, how much I taught them, or how well I thought I embraced who they were as people; if I didn't communicate in a way they could hear me it didn't matter.

Learning to communicate as a leader was a skill I needed to hone. Whether engaging an individual or the full team, I had to learn how to articulate a vision, set expectations, follow up, spotlight the team when we saw success, and take personal responsibility for the hiccups. Over time, I found that effective communication served as the measuring cups and spoons for my leadership recipe.

It allowed me to adjust the proportions of my ingredients based on what a person, team, or situation needed. Too much charisma and I was interpreted as phony. Too much advocacy for one teammate was favoritism. Too much focus on operational processes took away the fun in work, was interpreted as micro-managing, and ultimately resulted in the opposite of empowering my teammates.

I also learned that consistency mattered. It wasn't enough to just believe in or talk about empowerment. I had to invest time in teaching. A safe space was needed for learning, testing, and maybe even stumbling so people could get beyond their fear and gain confidence. I needed to seek opportunities for my teammates so they could develop new skills, access other leaders, and spotlight their strengths. As my career evolved, I found that ful-filling those needs was the focus of my job. Consistency in words and actions transformed my leadership recipe from a list of ingredients into an actual thing: my personal leadership dish.

The beauty of a recipe is that it can evolve. The ele-ments my leaders, mentors, and advocates built in me are foundational to the leadership dish I developed. But as my career evolved, exposure to new experiences and peo-ple introduced me to different perspectives (ingredients). Those insights influenced me. Like being introduced to pimente d'esplette and substituting it for paprika to add a little extra spice to a dish, colleagues and teammates showed me variations of traits and taught me the value of different situations requiring different types of leaders. As I work with and coach executives and leaders today,

I encourage them to focus on leveraging their strengths, help them identify and value the leadership traits in others, and help my clients know who they are. This opens the door to intentionally building the teams they need to execute their business goals. If they know and use their unique ingredients, they can refine their specific leadership recipes and execute an amazing dish.

This chapter began with two simple words: I am.

I am a communicator. Whether it's on stage to a large group, in a one-on-one conversation, or planning the rollout of a large initiative, I am energized by driving the message. I enjoy taking key parts of a message and translating them into something actionable. I know what I know and am not afraid to say, "I don't know." I get fired up delivering a vision or mission I believe in and making it come to life. This is probably my most visible ingredient.

I am an igniter, an ingredient that isn't evident immediately but reveals itself in time. I love creating and collaborating with others. A former employee once said, "There isn't a volunteer opportunity my boss doesn't like"—which is true! I believe in leading the change rather than being forced to change. I have a high tolerance for risk, we must *try*. It doesn't matter if it's a baby step or a giant leap—if I fail then I learn and keep moving.

I lead from a place of trust. There are skilled and

knowledgeable individuals in specialty roles on a team and they are needed. I trust that they are contributing toward the good of the business and I am committed to giving them what they need to do their jobs well. If it's a stretch project, I won't give it to you if I don't believe you can do it. If you need a flexible schedule to be your best, let's find a way to make it happen. If you need a safe place to be your whole self, to innovate without fear of retribution, to fail forward, I will provide it. A delicate ingredient, trust, can disintegrate if misused or disregarded.

I am a loud, optimistic, self-proclaimed entertainer and colorful personality who bring the fun factor to work! (And I put exclamation points everywhere even though my editor wants to cut them out!) What you see is what you get. And yes, I am *extra* which can be overwhelming for some people. But one of the highest compliments I received from a teammate was, "If Mylene is anything, it's consistent." As an ingredient, authenticity is my binding agent. It brings things together and was something I saw in every one of my leadership teachers. It's something I value and strive to bring to every space I am privileged to join.

I am an evolving leader. From early career learnings to my first HR team, to leading with senior executives at a Fortune 500 enterprise, to being in my Career 3.0

today; I continue to revisit, refine, and retool my recipe of leadership.

It's your turn. What is your recipe? Complete this sentence: I am...

EPILOGUE

I was thrilled to partner with these amazing women on this project. Their stories are inspiring and instructive. And although there was a range of experiences and leadership lessons learned, clear patterns emerged across the chapters.

Success. I wore out the thesaurus on this word and there are still over one hundred instances of its usage. Interestingly, there are few words that seem to capture the meaning of success accurately and the thesaurus failed me. Achievement, accomplishment, victory, and triumph don't resonate the same as success. Those words feel isolated or limited, where success seems broader. Much in the same way women approach leadership and success, we are interested in the success of the team or organization, not just ourselves. The word may be used too frequently in this work, but these women *were successful*. Sometimes the right word is the best word to use regardless of how many times it is said.

There was no shortage of passion and ambition in these pages. After reading this work, we must consider that ambition is incomplete, even unsatisfying, and may not create the same level of success as passion does. Ambition is a driver, especially early in one's career, but as people pound down a path established early in life, they often realize one of two things. Number one—I am not even interested or passionate about this. Or number two—is this all there is to life? Dedicating your time and energy to something without passion leads to dissatisfaction, even burn-out. Reflecting on our true passion and interest and allowing those things to shape our professional paths and our leadership styles creates a longer, healthier, and happier life and career.

This collection of successful leaders largely deployed a method of service leadership, putting their team members and responsibilities before themselves. They saw that their success would be achieved with an eye to the greater good, not just their individual accomplishments. Advocacy rang through each of these leader's styles, which was underpinned by their passion and drive. Each shared a measure of humility and willingness to learn. Their success was defined by the success of the team, the project, and the organization, and not their individual success.

These women are leaders. Successful and inspirational. Leaders.

DISCUSSION GUIDE

Head Up, Eyes Open, Heart Centered by Natalie Robinson
1. When did you know you were interested in leadership?
2. What are some important lessons you have learned about leadership in your career?
3. Come up with a leadership mantra like Head Up, Eyes Open, and Heart Centered for your style of leadership.

Decisions, Decisions, Decisions by Jennifer Pestikas
1. Describe an action you took as a leader that was unexpected, or above and beyond, and how it ultimately turned out. Are you glad you took those actions?
2. Describe a scenario where you leaned into a scenario or situation, did you achieve the desired results? Why or why not?
3. When is it imperative to "stick to your guns" and when is it wiser to let something go?

Winning on the Road by Ronicka Briscoe

1. What barriers or challenges have you faced? How have you overcome them?
2. How can we overcome rules or directional changes that are implemented in order to hamper our success?
3. Who is someone you admire? What are their key attributes?

Advocacy is Leadership by Mary Beth Ritchey

1. What examples do you have of *finding your voice?* What is an area of your career that you worked hard to be as good at as you are today?
2. Where else are leadership opportunities found?
3. If you could distill your leadership style down to one word, what would it be?

Life is Not a Straight Line by Churni Bhattacharya

1. Do you believe ambition will get you as far as passion?
2. Are you working in an area that aligns with your passion? Do you know what you are passionate about?
3. If you look back on successes from the past, do they look the same now as when you achieved them?

Meet the Moment by Shelia Higgs Burkhalter

1. What does "meeting the moment" mean to you?

2. Think about a personal experience where you or someone you know successfully met the moment. What strategies were employed, and what were the outcomes? What lessons can be drawn from these experiences?

3. Reflect on a time when you felt compelled to meet the moment and did not act. What held you back? What strategies can you use to own your seat at the table and speak up when needed?

4. Describe a time when you advocated for a certain circumstance and even with your hard work the decision did not go your way. How did you respond? Would you do it differently today?

5. What are ways we can prepare ourselves to *meet the moment*, when given the opportunity?

Let the Introverted Leader Fill Your Cup by Echelle Eady

1. What can we learn from introverted leaders? How is their leadership style different than extroverted leaders?

2. What are a few important things you do to fill your own cup to make sure you can fill the cups of others?

3. The concept of a graceful leader is not commonly discussed. How can we introduce more grace into our leadership styles and careers?

Bam! Pivot to Passion by Natalie Benamou

1. Have you had a life—or health-changing event that forced you to adjust your entire career? How did you manage it?

2. How do you forge ahead in new roles or assignments that you do not have a lot of experience in?

3. What would it take for you to go from a corporate job to starting and running your own business?

Authentic Leadership: Trust and Grace in Action by M.L. "Cissy" Petty

1. What professional and personal values shape your approach to leadership?

2. In what ways do you demonstrate your leadership authentically with your direct reports?

3. What tools do you use, and what guidance do you seek, to improve your leadership capabilities?

4. When you reflect on your leadership role, what team accomplishments are you most proud of and why?

5. For a moment, think like one of your staff members; how would they describe your leadership style? Is it consistent with how you see yourself?

Recipes of Leadership by Mylene Barizo

1. What societal or family environments may have shaped your career and leadership style?
2. What are the key ingredients to your personal leadership recipe?
3. Complete this sentence: I am….

ACKNOWLEDGEMENTS

This is the third Brave Women at Work project Jennifer and I have worked on. We jumped into a partnership with abandon and joy, and it has happily continued.

There is a consistent list of people we acknowledge that make all this work possible. First, we thank these amazing authors who joined us on our journey, shared their stories, and overcame the scary step of becoming authors. We thank these authors and the ones who came before, and the ones we know that will come after. Each of these women is part of the fabric and identity of Brave Women at Work.

Outside of us we have two team members. Tara is our designer. She is unparalleled in her swift delivery of beautiful materials, affordable pricing, and kindness. Dick Mueller is our copy editor whose sharp pen and piercing wit keeps our publications of the highest quality. Thank you to our small, but mighty team.

We thank our followers, supporters, and cheerleaders. Our Brave Women at Work and Hunter Street Press network is growing and each person who likes, shares, reposts, purchases, and writes reviews is invaluable to us. There are too many of you to list, but know that we see you, we appreciate you, and none of this would be possible without your efforts.

We thank our beautiful daughters, between the two of us, we are raising six incredible, confident, and powerful girls. These ladies never cease to amaze and inspire us. Hope's two grandsons can't be left out because they are future allies and partners in creating the Brave Women ecosystem.

Our life partners, John and Brad, are without a doubt the most patient, kind, and supportive partners anyone could find. As we traipse off with wild passion, time, and energy into our series of projects and business building, they love us, support us, and make sure we stop and drink a cup of coffee occasionally.

We always thank each other too because this partnership totally rocks! We collaborate, solve problems together; our businesses are growing together, and we are both deeply invested in each other's success and joy. Thank you Jennifer! Thank you Hope!

OTHER WORKS BY
HUNTER STREET PRESS

Brave Women at Work: Lessons in Confidence
By Jennifer Pestikas
Managing Editor Hope Mueller
Anthology Authors

Brave Women at Work: Lessons in Leadership
By Jennifer Pestikas
Managing Editor and Contributing Author Hope Mueller
Anthology Authors

Become, an Inspirational Journal
By Hope Mueller

Counting Hope, from conflict to confidence
By Hope Mueller

Hopey, from commune to corner office
By Hope Mueller

Printed in the USA
CPSIA information can be obtained
at www.ICGtesting.com
CBHW051747110924
14112CB00002B/2/J

9 781737 275138